Wake up...
Live the Life You Love,

In
Spirit

Wake up... Live the Life You Love, In Spirit

Little Seed Publishing, LLC
P.O. Box 4483
Laguna Beach, CA 92652

COPYRIGHT © 2005 by Global Partnership, LLC

Pre-Press Management by New Caledonian Press
Robert Valentine, Publications Director;
Lori Powell, Editorial Coordinator;
Rita Robinson, Accounts Manager.

Text Design: Wm. Gross Magee

Cover Design and Illustrations: Paul Romeo

Distributed by Global Partnership, LLC
100 North 6th Street, Suite A
Murray, KY 42071

Library of Congress Cataloguing-In-Publication Data
ISBN: 1-933063-02-5

$14.95 USA $24.95 Canada

Wake up... Live the Life You Love, In Spirit

Other books by Steven E

Wake Up...Live the Life You Love

Wake Up...Live the Life You Love, Second Edition

Wake Up...Shape Up...Live the Life You Love

*Wake Up...Live the Life You Love,
Inspirational How-to Stories*

Wake Up...Live the Life You Love, In Beauty

*Wake Up...Live the Life You Love,
Living on Purpose*

*Wake Up...Live the Life You Love,
Finding Your Life's Passion*

*Wake Up...Live the Life You Love,
Purpose, Passion, Abundance*

*Wake Up...Live the Life You Love,
Finding Personal Freedom*

*Wake Up...Live the Life You Love,
Seizing Your Success*

*Wake Up…Live the Life You Love,
Giving Gratitude*

*Wake Up…Live the Life You Love,
On the Enlightened Path*

For your free gift, go to: **www.wakeupand.com**

Wake up... Live the Life You Love, In Spirit

How would you like to be in the next book
with a fabulous group of best-selling authors?
Another Wake Up book is coming soon!

Visit: WakeUpLive.com

We would like to provide you with a free gift
to enhance this book experience. For your
free gift, please visit: WakeUpGift.com

Wake up... Live the Life You Love, In Spirit

Contents

Wake up... Live the Life You Love, In Spirit

For your free gift, go to: **www.wakeupand.com**

Wake up... Live the Life You Love, In Spirit

Wake up... Live the Life You Love, In Spirit

Wake up... Live the Life You Love, In Spirit

Embrace Silence
Dr. Wayne Dyer

You live in a noisy world, constantly bombarded with loud music, sirens, construction equipment, jet airplanes, rumbling trucks, leaf blowers, lawn mowers, and tree cutters. These man-made, unnatural sounds invade your sense and keep silence at bay.

In fact, you've been raised in a culture that not only eschews silence, but is terrified of it. The car radio must always be on, and any pause in conversation is a moment of embarrassment that most people quickly fill with chatter. For many, being alone in silence is pure torture.

The famous scientist Blaise Pascal observed, "All man's miseries derive from not being able to sit quietly in a room alone."

The Value of Silence

With Practice, you can become aware that there's a momentary silence in the space between your thoughts. In this silent space, you'll find the peace that you crave in your daily life. You'll never know that peace if you have no spaces between your thoughts.

The average person is said to have 60,000 separate thoughts every day. With so many thoughts, there are almost no gaps. If you could reduce that number by half, you would open up an entire world of possibilities for yourself. For it is when you merge in the silence and become one with it that you reconnect to your source and know the peacefulness that some call God. "Be still and know that I am God," says it so beautifully in Psalms of the Old Testament. The key words are "still" and "know."

Wake up... Live the Life You Love, In Spirit

"Still" actually means silence. Mother Theresa described silence and its relationship to God by saying, "God is the friend of Silence. See how nature—trees, grass—grows in silence; see the stars, the moon and the sun—how they move in silence. We need silence to be able to touch souls." This includes your soul!

It's really the space between the notes that makes the music you enjoy so much. Without the spaces, all you would have is one continuous noisy note. Everything that's created comes out of silence. Your thoughts emerge from the nothingness of silence. Your words come out of this void. Your very essence emerged from emptiness.

Those who will supersede us are waiting in the vast void. All creativity requires some stillness. Your sense of inner peace depends on spending some of your life energy in silence to recharge your batteries and remove tension and anxiety, thus reacquainting you with the joy of knowing God and feeling closer to all of humanity. Silence reduces fatigue and allows you to experience your own creative juices.

The second word in the Old Testament observation, "know," refers to making your personal and conscious contact with God. To know God is to banish doubt and become independent of others' definitions and descriptions of God. Instead, you have your own personal knowing. And, as Melville reminded us so poignantly, "God's one and only voice is silence."

❧ Dr. Wayne Dyer

Wake up... Live the Life You Love, In Spirit

Live an Inspired Life
Michael O'Rourke

As the CEO of a beauty care company and a hairdresser for over 40 years, I've been privileged to study human nature from different perspectives. At the height of my hairdressing career, I spent an average of 14 hours a day, six days a week in the act of making someone feel beautiful. As I look back on it, it's an amazing gift. And despite that it's been physically grueling, I wouldn't have changed my destiny even if I could. Imagine getting up every day doing something you love, getting paid very well, and making people feel beautiful. I'm the luckiest guy in the world.

I've been sought out, time and again, as an opinion leader on the subject of beauty. I guess, when you spend 40 years doing a thing, people think you ought to know. I bet I've heard the words, "what makes her so beautiful?" at least 10,000 times in my life. People seem to believe there's a magic formula, a cheek-to-chin contour, a hairstyle or lip color that defines that radiant glow that undefined allure, that certain something. I never gave it a second thought, never granted an interview or even shared my perspective until I was asked to write this article. In retrospect, I should have analyzed this a long time ago, but I was just too busy taking in all the beauty.

So here's the answer. The beauty secret of the most beautiful women on the planet is that they "live an inspired life." That's it. The allure these women possess is magnetic. Their eyes mesmerize, their smile seems to open heaven. You can study their features and fixate on their every move, yet their beauty is undefined. It's inexplicable. You can't put your finger on it, but

Wake up... Live the Life You Love, In Spirit

you know it's something. Well, it's something all right, and that something is spirit. These beauties are living an inspired life.

The word "inspiration" is derived from the Latin root *spirare,* meaning "spirit:" to breathe, to give life—the breath of God. Is it any wonder these women are so attractive? They are formed from "the breath of God." So why are they "the chosen ones," you might ask? Because they choose to be the chosen ones; they choose to lead and live an inspired life—and you can too.

If you want to make the leap from *tired to inspired,* then it will take focus. It will take courage, creativity, and commitment. Each morning when you awake, make it your mission to allow life to inspire you. Let the beauty of the sunrise astound you; drink in every color until you can't take in anymore. Allow the crisp morning air to brush away any sorrow as it brushes up against your skin. Breathe in every lush fragrance from every flower, and release any toxin holding you back. Let the sound of laughter drown out the noise of your tired aching joints. Find something magical in every moment you observe and let your passions lead you. Learn to listen to the voice of spontaneity and live your life as you want to be remembered.

Living an inspired life transcends external motivation. It's not being motivated to do great things. It's doing great things because you are inspired. People are motivated mostly by fear. Inspiration, on the other hand, is derived from spirit. People that live an inspired life do so out of love. It's a "no strings attached" perspective. Live. Love. Dare. Dream. Do. It's pretty simple when you think about it.

To all of you reading this tome I leave this simple Zulu statement: Ubuntu. It means "to go or to do things with a good heart." How's that for inspiration?

Ↄ Michael O'Rourke

Wake up... Live the Life You Love, In Spirit

Why Am I Here?
Deepak Chopra

From an Interview with Dr. R. Winn Henderson

The majority of people on earth are unfulfilled or unhappy because they do not have a purpose or a mission. As a part of the human species, we seek purpose and meaning; we laugh, and we are aware of our mortality (that one day we will die). This is what distinguishes us from other creatures. Laughter, mortality and purpose become three important, crucial questions. We search for meaning—a deep significance to life.

Why am I here? Why have I been placed on the earth? We've been placed on earth to make a difference in life itself and in others' lives. In order to make a difference, we must find what we are good at, like to do, and benefits others.

We all have a mission, and my mission in life is to understand and explore consciousness and its various expressions and also to share that with anyone who's interested in doing the same. It boils down to understanding the mechanics of healing, the rule of love. I would say to put it very simply, my mission is to love, to heal, to serve and to begin the process of transforming both for myself and for those that I come in contact with.

As part of my mission, I founded The Chopra Center. My mission: to educate health professionals, patients and the general public on the connection between the relationship of mind, body, and spirit and healing. I teach people how to find their inner-self (most people have lost touch with theirs). When we find our inner-self, we find the wisdom that our bodies can be

Wake up... Live the Life You Love, In Spirit

wonderful pharmacies—creating wonderful drugs—you name it, the human body can make it in the right dose, at the right time, for the right organ without side effects.

The body is a network of communication. Our thoughts influence everything that happens in our body. The problem is many people automatically assume, "All I have to do is think positively, and everything will be fine." Because many assume this, they become unnatural and pretend everything is okay.

One must go beyond that; one must experience silence. It is when one experiences silence, healing energies become involved and a balance is created. Psalms 46:10 says, "Be still and know that I am God." When the body is silent, it knows how to repair itself.

Pursuing my mission gives me fulfillment. It makes me whole. It makes me feel that I will continue to do what I have been doing. If I had all the time and money in the world, this is what I would choose to do. It gives me joy and a connection to the creative bar of the universe. I have realized that the pursuit of my goals is the progressive expansion of happiness.

Pursue your goals and find your happiness, wholeness, and balance in this world.

෴ Deepak Chopra, M.D.

Blessed or Stressed?

David Laughray

*A*re you stressed? Does something in your life seem out of control? Are you experiencing an emotional upset, a mental block, a physical challenge, or a relationship problem? If so, there is one solution that always works. Unfortunately, most people are not aware of this simple solution. This is why stress is in epidemic proportions in our country today.

I am about to tell you the secret to overcoming stress. I have shared this with thousands of people for over 25 years and it always works. This one idea will dramatically change your life from this point forward. Ready! Here it is. At any given point in time you can choose to feel stressed or you can choose to feel blessed. That's right. It has nothing to do with outside circumstances. It has only to do with "inside" circumstances. You can choose to focus inwardly and tap into the Spirit of Love that is always available.

When you choose the Spirit of Love, it will direct you, guide you, heal you, and lift you out of every "negative" situation. You become automatically blessed. No habit, anxiety, doubt, fear, or worry has power over the Spirit of Love.

Now I am going to tell you another secret. You don't have to wait until you feel stress to contact the Spirit of Love. That is what most people do. They wait until they feel so much stress they have to do something about it. Then they turn to the Spirit of Love in order to feel blessed. Although this is better than staying in stress, there is a better way.

The better way is to develop a lifestyle in which the Spirit of Love becomes so natural that it takes over before stress even

has a chance. Here are three strategies that I teach that have changed lives.

First of all, **Start Your Day with Love**. When you wake up, open your heart and remind yourself who you really are. Know that you are a living expression of God's Infinite Spirit. Remind yourself that you are unique. You have a gift to give to your world. Then, give thanks in advance for a successful day. See it filled with loving relationships, prosperous transactions, and irrevocable joy.

Next, **Live Your Day with Love**. Live from your heart. A major cause of stress is doing what everyone else is doing when your heart does not really want to do it. Stop falling into daily routines out of default. Living from your heart means you choose a lifestyle that is true for you and your family. You make important decisions because they resonate with your values. When you live from your heart, you trust your instincts more than the pressures of the outside world. You are able to listen and obey "the still small voice" that knows what to do and how to do it. Also, as you go through your day, never miss an opportunity to say, "I love you." Those three words can mean so much to people. It makes them feel good. It reminds them that they are not alone and that you care. It also reminds you of your capacity to feel and express who you really are. Living your day with love takes place when you decide that how you live your life is more important than the results you seek.

Finally, **End Your Day with Love**. The moments that really stand out are the ones that touch your heart. Spend time remembering them. Spend time in gratitude for all the things you have and the gifts of love you have received in your life. It is so tempting to spend time hoping things will get better later, looking forward to a promotion, special events, or vacations. While these are great things to anticipate, if we focus too much on them we miss out on the incredible special events that happen on a regular basis, the ones we take for granted. For me, it is combing my daughter's hair; it is when she tells me how

Wake up... Live the Life You Love, In Spirit

much she loves me. It is not the big wedding that stands out in my life; it is the first time my wife told me she loved me. I am sure you have many examples in your own life, countless seemingly small things that add up to a life filled with love. End your day thinking on these things.

You will soon discover that your life is filled with passion and joy for no apparent reason. It just is. I know that the Spirit of Love is blessing you this very instant. So say, "Yes!" to the joy and passion of life surging through you now.

                                             ↆ David Laughray

Wake up... Live the Life You Love, In Spirit

Wake up... Live the Life You Love, In Spirit

Tapping into the Flow of Opulence
Terry Cole-Whittaker, D.D.

*L*ife is good when we understand how it works. Those who have taken the time and energy to find out about the laws and principles of successful living and the Infinite Creative Power within them are called extraordinary, fortunate, and highly successful.

I first learned about this amazing power and how to use it by reading a book about a man who tapped the secrets of the universe. His amazing way of life intrigued me and I was inspired by what he easily accomplished simply by accessing this infinite storehouse of wisdom, bliss, power, and genius. I thought, "If he could produce magnificent pieces of art, bring forth inventions, become highly fortunate, become an expert in anything he attempted, create brilliantly written books of prose and poetry, and be highly respected, then why couldn't I fulfill my heart's desires?"

Right then and there I decided to put his philosophy into practice and find out what I could accomplish. I am happy to say that, by applying these principles and continuing my studies of sacred and practical wisdom, I have been able to accomplish anything and everything I set out to do, and so can anyone.

To be the successful person I am talking about there are three important principles to follow. The first principle is the acceptance of a higher intelligence and power, which is the source of supreme bliss and opulence. The scriptures of the great religions tell us that we are to realize that there is one God, one Power, one absolute Source and Substance of all. Call

Wake up... Live the Life You Love, In Spirit

this Presence and Power whatever you desire, but by whatever name, It remains what It is and always will be.

Why is this important to accept? Understanding that there is a supernatural Power that is in, around, and through all of us at all times gives us God-awareness. A spiritually intelligent person has the edge, for he or she is without fear, completely confident, relentlessly motivated and enthused, and able to receive whatever is needed and wanted by mentally and emotionally unifying with, and thus drawing from, this Source. Those who are on the elevated spiritual platform are virtually without limits, they can see their possibilities far beyond what they have experienced or known before.

The second principle is to open your mind to your possibilities. By unifying your mind with the Universal Mind, or what some call the Mind of God, you make yourself a branch office of the opulent storehouse of whatever is available anywhere. The way to do this is to remember that there is one Divine Mind of which your mind is a channel. Open the flood gates of your mind to receive the Divine influx of what is available in this Universal Intelligence and allow it to bring forth the solutions, answers, energy, ideas, and resources you need to attain your goals.

By asking for and accepting with absolute faith the support of this supernatural Power, the right people, ideas, and opportunities come to us effortlessly and our path is made smooth and joyful. Those who are expert in unifying their minds with the Divine Mind easily attract wealth.

The third principle is Love. By the right use of love, you will naturally prosper and be happy. Love means working to please and make others happy. Pleasing your clients guarantees that they will continue to purchase your goods and services. Bringing joy to your loved ones makes a happy home in which good fortune will bless you with all forms of wealth. Geniuses love their work so much that they see their work as play. Loving is a feeling that is in our true nature, but just as a seed must be watered to grow, we must actively give it in order to receive it and make it grow. Love is God, and we enter into

Wake up... Live the Life You Love, In Spirit

the realm of opulence when we love. By being in the habit of seeing and loving the Divine in every living entity, and by acknowledging Its presence everywhere, we will surely find heaven on earth.

ༀ Terry Cole-Whittaker D.D.

Wake up... Live the Life You Love, In Spirit

Wake up... Live the Life You Love, In Spirit

The Entrepreneurial COMPASS
Paul Romeo

I have found seven keys to help you in your quest to reach your goals and enjoy the freedom of a successful business. The turning of each key may seem simple, but you will require all the strength of your spirit to open the doors now closed to you.

Do you own a business? Have you ever heard the expression, "Can't see the forest for the trees?" Are you too busy working *in* your business to work *on* it? If so, you might find the "Entrepreneurial C.O.M.P.A.S.S." a useful navigation aid in your quest to reach your goals.

It's a simple but effective formula I developed during my years as an entrepreneur in starting, running, and selling several successful companies.

Just like an explorer uses a compass to keep from getting lost, the Entrepreneurial C.O.M.P.A.S.S. can help keep you from getting lost in the details. If used daily, it will enable you to step back, re-focus, and stay headed toward your business goals. Even though it is for entrepreneurs, it can be easily adapted to help you in the pursuit of your personal goals.

Write the following C.O.M.P.A.S.S. points on an index card or small piece of paper to keep in your wallet or post next to your computer. Glance at it several times throughout the day; ultimately, memorizing is best.

Here are the parts of the Entrepreneurial C.O.M.P.A.S.S

C = <u>Competence and Commitment</u>—Ultimate freedom and success comes with doing what you love. However, doing what you love in business is not always enough. You must also, be competent at it; successful people are both passionate and competent. The "C" also stands for Commitment, an

Wake up... Live the Life You Love, In Spirit

equally important ingredient in reaching any goal. Imagine what would happen if Sir Edmund Hillary, the first man to reach the summit of Mt. Everest, had not been committed to reaching the top. He would have given up on his first attempt. Remember *Competency* and *Commitment*.

O = **Outlook**—The dictionary defines "outlook" as a "future expectation, and the act of looking out." You should have a clear vision of what your business goals should be. In fact, you should write them down, and include as much detail as possible about your vision and goals. Outlook is also linked to *attitude*. Replace negative thinking with a positive outlook. You'll be surprised how powerful a positive outlook really is. A positive outlook and clear goals are critical.

M = **Marketing**—Marketing is just as important as your product or service. One of the biggest mistakes new entrepreneurs make is not putting enough focus on marketing. Good marketing is the fuel that keeps businesses running.

P = **Prioritize**—Put first things first. Create a daily task list of those activities that are directly involved in reaching your primary goals. Are you doing work just to keep busy, or are you doing activities that will help reach your goals? Prioritize your list; then focus and complete each action.

A = **Action**—Nothing happens without action. The world is full of dreamers who never take action. If you want massive results, create massive action plans and then follow through. But here's the real secret to action, it needs to be *correct* action.

S = **Systematize**—Systems enable successful businesses to grow and endure. Most successful businesses have systems for each part of their business: systems for order processing, systems for manufacturing, systems for selling, etc. Take franchises for an example of a successful business model. One reason why franchises have lower failure rates than traditional business start-ups is that every part of their business is systematized to be *duplicated*. You can do the same for your business.

S = **Start**—Starting is one of the most important keys of the C.O.M.P.A.S.S. What does "Start" mean? It means, "Don't *procrastinate*." Don't procrastinate; take action. Don't procrastinate;

Wake up... Live the Life You Love, In Spirit

decisions that need to be made. Procrastination is a poison that will prevent you from moving your business—and your life forward, and it can ruin your chances for success. "Start" is your antidote.

That's it; seven keys to help keep you pointed in the right direction when building a successful business—the Entrepreneurial C.O.M.P.A.S.S. It shows the path that leads, inevitably, to your personal freedom.

ᗡ Paul Romeo

Wake up... Live the Life You Love, In Spirit

A Knock at the Door;
A Beckon, and 'Come with me'
Glenn R. Mosley, Ph.D.

*A*t ten years of age, I told my mother I couldn't attend the
family church anymore. We lived in the country and because
my closest friends were our animals, she didn't have to worry
that I would get into trouble staying by myself. She agreed to
let me stay home. I didn't attend church anywhere for three
years and then, on my own, I began attending several different
churches. I visited two Catholic churches, a Jewish Temple, a
Jewish Synagogue, and 26 Protestant denominations. When I
was 14, my mother quit the family church (her father had been
a farmer and itinerant preacher in that church) and she also
began attending other churches.

On the third Sunday that my mother and I attended a
Unity Church, something happened to me. As the congregation stood to sing, "I'll go where you want me to go, dear
Lord," I could hardly sing for two reasons. I had a lump in
my throat and I couldn't read the words through my tears. My
mother looked at me and smiled and nodded her head. Neither
of us spoke of that experience for three weeks. When we did,
I admitted that at that moment, I began considering becoming a Unity minister. I had not been looking for a profession
in the ministry. I wanted to live a life I could love, a life of
spirit, a pursuit of spirituality that I could use in my daily life.
I thought I had my career path figured out. But on that day
in church, I felt as though some part of me was knocking at
the door of my consciousness. When I answered, there stood
that part of me, smiling, with two beckoning fingers, saying,
"Come with me."

Wake up... Live the Life You Love, In Spirit

I wasn't accustomed to having my hard-won decisions lightly overturned. When I was graduated from high school, I proceeded to college to study microbiology. I was preparing for a career in medicine, although I was wavering between medicine and ministry. After college, at the ripe old age of 19, I still was unsure about what professional school to choose, so I took a position in industry for about three years. During that time I became an assistant department head in wage and salary administration. Again, I was beckoned, "Come with me." I decided to attend ministerial school over medical school. I went to see my supervisor to turn in my resignation. He laughed and told me that he had just seen the plant superintendent to tender his resignation and that I had already been approved to replace him (at twice my salary). Again, a part of me knocked at the door, I answered, and there was a beckoning, "Come with me."

At times my life's path seemed clear and certain. At other times it was neither, but I knew that I would need to remain open to further guidance. I would need to be ready and willing to change plans, even at a moment's notice. Upon graduation from ministerial school, I was asked where I wanted to go. I answered, "East." I was from Ohio and ministerial school was near Kansas City, Missouri; I was thinking of east as Toledo, Ohio or Pittsburgh, Pennsylvania. Then came another knock at the door, a beckon, and, "Come with me." My first ministry was in Flushing, New York. While there I taught a class in Huntington, New York. Another beckon and, "Come with me," resulted in my pioneering a ministry in Huntington while serving in Flushing. There followed an interim ministry in Des Moines, Iowa, an associate position in Manhattan, New York, and two long-term ministries in Detroit, Michigan and Akron, Ohio.

Each time, just when I thought everything had settled down, I recall answering a knock at the door, being beckoned, and hearing, "Come with me." What I thought was surely the last such call came when I was recruited to apply to become the

Wake up... Live the Life You Love, In Spirit

President of the Association of Unity Churches, International. That was twenty years ago and the call is back again. The "Come with me" message is saying "the life of spirit you love" is to be continued in field ministry, in a church. And who knows where else?

                           ↄ Glenn R. Mosley, Ph.D.

Wake up... Live the Life You Love, In Spirit

What Are You Afraid of? You Can Transform Your Fear into Faith
Dr. Barbara King

I am often asked to speak, write, and counsel people on the issue of how to handle fear. If we can learn to focus on God and not on fear, we can develop a stronger faith and stop coddling our fears. Webster defines fear as "an unpleasant, often strong emotion caused by anticipation or awareness of danger." This indicates that fear is man-made.

When we allow some object, other person, or situation to become so large in our consciousness, that we become fearful of it, we lose control of ourselves. We allow the magnitude of the fear to become bigger than God. The fear, the thing we dread, seems to be in total command of us. We don't have to be afraid, because fear is an emotion, and emotions are ours to control.

When we allow fear to take control we are denying that we are one with God. We are refusing to allow God to show us His plan for our lives.

What are you afraid of? All of us have experienced the emotion of fear: fear of taking a vacation by traveling on a commercial airplane; fear of failing a test in a class needed for graduation; fear of jumping into the deep water of a swimming pool; fear of taking a walk in the woods and encountering a snake; fear of not earning enough money to cover the bills; fear of dying; fear of speaking in public; fear of not being good enough to meet someone else's expectations. The *Bible* says, "God has not given us the spirit of fear, but of power, and of love, and of a sound mind." The power of the Spirit of the liv-

Wake up... Live the Life You Love, In Spirit

ing God that is within us, can overcome fear. How do we call this power forth?

We can seek to be a balanced person.

We are threefold beings; we are spirit, mind, and body. It is important to nourish all three dimensions. We can maintain a balance in our spiritual lives by practicing the presence of God; by nourishing our minds (the intellectual and creative aspects of our brains) through a variety of academic, educational, and cultural activities; and by taking care of our body temples through proper nutrition, rest, and physical activity.

When was the last time you read a good book? Heard an inspiring sermon? Shared a meal with a homeless family? Attended a performance at the theatre? Been to a music concert? Enrolled in a continuing education class? Fasted from heavy food? Walked up a flight of stairs instead of taking the elevator? Rested for a day or perhaps piddled for an hour?

We can expect every day to be the best.

We can train ourselves to expect the best. Living with this expectation creates the outcome for good in our lives. Realizing that the words we speak are power tools of good, we can speak positively rather than negatively.

Have you met people who thrive on negativity? When you listen to the key words in their vocabularies, you realize that you hear only words such as "no, never, none, nothing, can't, wouldn't, shouldn't, couldn't, won't, and don't." When we expect every day to be the best, our vocabulary will contain positive words.

We can be decisive and stand by our decisions.

Chronic worriers are not able to make a decision and stick with it. We sometimes blame external factors for our not making a decision to reach our goals. Have you ever declined an invitation because *you didn't have anything to wear?* Declined to join the church choir because *you couldn't sing?* Felt unsure about applying for a scholarship because *you weren't smart enough?* Hesitated about trying out for the basketball team because *you weren't tall enough?* Did not plan to take that dream trip because *you didn't have the money?* The external factors are our fears that have taken control of our decisions or lack of decision.

We can take action.

It has been said that faith without works is dead, and works without faith is just as dead. People often struggle to take action after a decision has been made because of fear—taking a certain job, buying a home, establishing a relationship, ending a relationship, or seeking a mate. To reach our goals, we must act on our decisions and not allow our fears to hold us back.

Seek balance, expect the best, be decisive, and take action. You will find that you can overcome your fears and find the strength and power that is within.

ᕤ Dr. Barbara King

Wake up... Live the Life You Love, In Spirit

Shifting to Spirit's Abundance
Rev. Jim Chandler

I believe that I was born into a life of privilege. For many, being a person of "privilege" means to be born into an environment of abundant wealth and power. For me, it is a life where everything anyone ever needs is provided for abundantly throughout his or her entire lifetime. For me to understand that I was living a life of privilege came to me through a series of powerful lessons and useful experiences, unexpected new opportunities and empowering new choices. The discovery of the privileged path I followed was not always appreciated at the time. There were insignificant events which revealed pathways to success and others which healed past wounds, or opened to something I desired but had no idea was possible.

After my parents divorced when I was 9 years old, my mother had the task of raising three young children on a modest secretarial income. My siblings and I became latch-key kids. There were drawbacks, but there were also benefits. We developed self–discipline, responsibility, confidence, pride in our work, and dedication which empowered us. We were assigned household chores and we were each responsible for creating a way to earn money and contribute toward our personal expenses. My job, at the age of nine, was a daily newspaper route.

By the time I turned 16 the one small route had expanded to multiple routes where I learned valuable skills that would later help me in business. On my 16th birthday I was hired by a local discount superstore to bag groceries, while continuing my schooling. I soon was promoted to cashier and then to the housewares department. Next I was promoted to manager of the record department, and camera department, and right up the ladder. At the age of 18, while attending the University of

Wake up... Live the Life You Love, In Spirit

Arizona, I was given the opportunity to move to Los Angeles, to be a buyer, and to begin my move up the corporate ladder.

By the time I was 21, the company was purchased by a larger corporation and my position was eliminated. The organization I had trusted for my future had let me down. I soon found that I was "unemployable." No one wanted to hire a national buyer for a retail chain who was only 21 years old. I was too young for my experience, and too experienced for my age. I was forced to create a new path.

A friend of mine was quite a horticultural expert, and I had a business background that went all the way back to the age of nine. Together we formed a horticultural supply company which soon began to grow and prosper. Six years later at the time of the first oil embargo the business failed. We had to lay everyone off and close the business.

I had started over before; I could do it again. I had always been interested in automobiles, so I asked the owner of a local dealership where I had done business if he had any openings on the sales staff. I started out as a part-time salesman, and within a couple of months was his sales manager. This gave me an "employable" occupation, so I decided to make a change. I loved to ski, so on the promise of a position with a large dealership in Denver, I left Los Angeles and moved to Colorado.

Colorado was good to me. I gradually moved up to selling more prestigious (and profitable) vehicles, such as Mercedes Benz, Maserati, and Lotus, and I was back on the path to success and prosperity. I had a big house, two luxury cars, a pickup, and several motorcycles. I had all the trappings of abundance, but deep inside something was missing. Then one day, something happened that changed my life. The change was brought about be a very unusual source and through a most unlikely person.

I remember it clearly. I was the manager of an exotic car dealership, leaning against the hood of a red Maserati in our showroom. As I gazed out the window, my eyes landed on a homeless man across the street rummaging through the garbage.

Wake up... Live the Life You Love, In Spirit

I thought of a phrase we all have heard many times: "There but for the grace of God go I." Then I thought, "No, that could never be me." It's not that I didn't have compassion for the man, it's just that I couldn't see myself in that situation. It just couldn't be. Suddenly, I realized something about my life. I had had many, many failures, but I had always been provided for. There were times when money was tight, but I was never broke. When I failed I was never homeless. No matter how broke I may have felt, somehow, from somewhere, food, money, or a new opportunity came into my life. Maybe that's what prosperity and "privilege" is really about. Not the Maserati, or the house, or the money, but a deep understanding, a deep sense, a conscious connection and understanding that the source has always been there, something I didn't have to create.

We never know who will be our teachers in life; where we will find that special experience, or special lesson to transform our thinking. My teacher was an unaware homeless man, searching through the garbage. The lesson he gave me was that until I can hold it in my mind, until I can embrace the possibility, until it could be an option for me, I need not fear poverty or failure. It is no longer about working hard, or how much I can produce. It has nothing to do with the business I am in, or the occupation I claim. Businesses fail. Things happen. As long as I find it impossible to envision poverty in my life, I have nothing to fear.

Not long after that experience, I left the automobile business and went to ministerial school. I created a new kind of church based on service and community involvement. I now fill much of my time working with nonprofit organizations, some of which provide medical services and basic needs for people like my homeless teacher.

I have a smaller house and more modest automobiles, yet my life is more prosperous than ever. Through the church and the other organizations, I am able to help transform lives.

If we can trust our prosperity to Spirit, we can live a new abundant life, a life no longer dedicated to work, but to an

Wake up... Live the Life You Love, In Spirit

expression of our passion. We look less at what we have accumulated and more at how we have empowered lives through the giving nature of Spirit. Abundance is the nature of Spirit; it flows to us and through us from many diverse channels. We become a channel through which our conscious flows to others. Prosperity is the nature of creation. It is our divine birthright. By accepting it, we become a source for others. It is our divine birthright as a "privileged child" of the Universe.

ᗧ Rev. Jim Chandler

Joy Is in My Hands
Dr. Kathy Hearn

I have long been impressed by the ways in which the universe
conspires to deliver to me the messages I need. For the most
part, I have graduated from the "2-by-4" experiences of my
early days on the spiritual path—those abrupt and uncomfortable learning episodes that arrive in the guise of the conse-
quences of unskilled behavior and less-than-conscious choices
and actions. More recently, thankfully, I receive messages
through kinder and gentler channels. Several times, precious
instances of awakening have come through hummingbirds. I
assumed my relationship with the tiny creatures was unique to
me until I began sharing this story. I discovered that these fast-
winged emissaries of spiritual communication visit many.

In the Native American tradition of animal medicine, hummingbirds are symbols and messengers of joy. My first close
encounter with one of them came six months into a time of
deep and dark personal loss and grief that followed the sudden ending of my 25-year marriage. I had gone to sit on the
balcony of the lovely large home that was soon to be sold, des-
perately seeking connection with something in and around me
other than pain. As I looked out on the green of a lush hillside,
a hummingbird flew right in front of my face and hovered
there for several seconds, the vibration of its wings saying to
me, "You know, there is still joy." I laughed out loud at such a
direct communiqué, and that moment marked a turning point
for me. From that day on I made a steady climb back to the
light and sense of my new life.

Four years later brought the next installment of the unfold-
ing message. I entered my bedroom one day to see my cat

Wake up... Live the Life You Love, In Spirit

reclining in a sunspot, intently looking at something. I followed her gaze to the window and saw there a hummingbird, which had flown in a door that opens onto a deck of blooming flowers. As its wings hummed and beat in vain against the panes, I lowered the window to facilitate its escape. The hummingbird only followed the window down. There was nothing to do to help but take this little bird in my hands and carry it outside. To my great surprise it did not struggle, but lay very still in my cupped palms. I had several moments to marvel at its colors of iridescent green and fuchsia, its needlelike beak. One small bead of an eye, black like obsidian, stared into mine. Suspended in time, we two species merely regarded each other, both of us equally astonished. A message sparked in my mind: "Joy is in my hands." As this incredible joy filled me, I understood that "<u>My</u> joy is in <u>my</u> hands."

My joy is in my hands, no one else's, just as your joy is in yours. If there is to be joy in our lives, it is up to each one of us to experience it in the ordinary as well as extraordinary moments of time, to express it through giving ourselves fully to life, and to celebrate it in our sharing with each other. More than that, Joy is a Quality of God, part of the Essence of the Divine. It is, therefore, an essential and unalterable part of our own being. Joy arises from within, and is not dependent upon people, places, or things being a certain way. Joy cannot be taken from us; only we can steal it from ourselves. But it can be resisted and denied, lost and then recovered. "Joy is a sure sign of the Presence of God," someone wise wrote. More challenging is the statement by Paramahansa Yogananda, "It is possible under all circumstances to be joyful." It is good spiritual practice to live this.

I am grateful to the winged messengers of joy that surround the house I live in now. Most mornings I awaken to hear their odd little hummingbird chirping sounds - reminding me to remember that Joy is what I am; that my life is Joy.

ख Dr. Kathy Hearn

Wake up... Live the Life You Love, In Spirit

No, Virginia, There Is No "Santa God"
Dr. Michelle Medrano

I was seven years old and I had it all figured out: God and Santa Claus were brothers and they were the sole creators of the universe. In Sunday school I was told that if I was a good girl and obeyed the *Bible* and God's son, Jesus, I would go to heaven. Comparably, my parents and culture told me that if I was a good girl and did what I was told, every Christmas Santa Claus would reward me with gifts and goodies. I concluded that these two old men—with white beards, great power, and splendid magic—must be related. After all, they were similar in appearance and both demanded that I be good.

I also believed in the Easter bunny. My first spiritual crisis unfolded the night I willed myself to stay awake to meet him. I waited patiently, my heart beating with anticipation of the miracle I was about to see. But instead of the Easter bunny, I saw my mother sneaking into my room with a colorful basket of candy. I was dumbfounded. If she was the Easter bunny, I thought, could she also be Santa Claus? One day, riding with my mother in the car, I asked her, "Mom, are you really Santa Claus?"

"What do you think, Shelly?" she responded.

The jig was up. The "benevolent brothers" story I had devised, my foundation explaining life, lost its meaning. Like in the 1939 film *The Wizard of Oz*, when Toto pulls the curtain back to reveal not a great wizard but an ordinary man controlling levers, I had pulled back the curtain and exposed a cosmic charade. Adults had lied about Santa to manipulate me into being good. And, if they had lied about Santa, then they must

Wake up... Live the Life You Love, In Spirit

have lied about God, too. If there was no Santa, there must be no God: at least, not the God they had told me about. From that point on I vowed not to believe adults again. I would not believe priests or nuns or my mom and dad about spiritual matters. Yet, as I grew older, my mind and my heart could feel the universal heart beat. I could see the miracle of life in the faces of my little sister and brother. The birth of kittens was amazing. I saw the magnificence of trees and mountains. All the beauty I witnessed was evidence that there must be a Creator. God had to be real. When I was 13 my mother and I cautiously walked into the New Thought/Religious Science Church at Mile Hi Church in Denver, Colorado. I immediately felt at home. The teachings there opened my soul to new and exciting possibilities. My old ideas and bitterness about God slowly dissolved. In this new spiritual setting, I saw that I was being called to embrace a larger idea of Spirit in my life. A new idea of God based firmly in my own inner recognition dawned. I sometimes had moments of doubt as I peered into the depths of the miracle of life. As I awakened to Spirit, I discovered a God born of unity, oneness, and love.

I am now a grown woman and a minister in the powerful faith tradition of Religious Science. I see people struggle, as I did, with the idea of "Santa God." "Santa God" represents patriarchy, judgment, ego, and pain. He represents a "Big Daddy in the sky" who can make it all better. The problem is that He doesn't seem to be trying very hard to make it all better, and we wonder why pain, problems, starvation, violence, and a whole host of other problems exist.

Like a child clinging to the myth of Santa, millions still cling to the myth of the "Big Daddy." Their prayers often become, as Bishop John Shelby Spong suggests, "adult letters to Santa Claus." For many, releasing this myth is very painful. For others, this release brings a great sense of freedom and joy, and its power enables them to face the challenges of the world.

Our flourishing as spiritual beings demands that we step fully into our Unity. Awakening to the Eternal Spirit calls us

Wake up... Live the Life You Love, In Spirit

all to surrender our belief in "Santa God" and continually embrace a grander concept of the living universe. No, there is no "Santa God." But if we awaken to the oneness of Spirit, we can receive universal gifts and goodies, every day.

೭ Dr. Michelle Medrano

Wake up... Live the Life You Love, In Spirit

Wake up... Live the Life You Love, In Spirit

Spiritual Medicine
Rev. Kathy McCall

When I was in ministerial school I killed a deer. This was not a prerequisite one would expect for the ministry, but it woke me up and changed my life. I was driving my six-year-old son Justin to his daycare on my way to school very early one morning. While my son slept in the front seat I was, ironically, practicing aloud a lecture that I was to give that morning on death and dying. At that moment a large deer jumped into the headlights and I had time only to brace myself for the impact.

It sent us flying off the road into an embankment, which probably saved us from the traffic behind. Aside from a slight bump on his head, Justin was okay, and I was not physically injured. The deer, however, fell and with great effort rose, fell, and rose again, about five times as it staggered all the way to my car window, where it looked directly into my eyes, collapsed one last time, and then died. Overwhelmed and trembling, I put my head down on the steering wheel and sobbed.

Later I was told by the sheriff that the particular ten-point buck I hit was the largest deer he had ever seen. The experience taught me some basic truths which I believe are relevant for everyone: *1) The meaning we give to the events in our life is essential; 2) It is important to let go of false beliefs and embrace truth, and; 3) All life is sacred.*

I came to these realizations because of what occurred following the accident. Several nights later, due to unusual circumstances involving a church dinner party that was progressing from one house to another, a shamanic facilitator ended up at my house. (Shamans are the medicine men or women of indigenous tribes who seek to guide and heal through contact

Wake up... Live the Life You Love, In Spirit

with "non-ordinary" reality; a shamanic facilitator, though not necessarily a shaman, is one who practices shamanism.) This particular woman had expertise in guiding people on "dream journeys," and she led me through this meditative experience to ask the deer why it died. The answer that I received was that the deer had "died for my sins!" It gave an entirely new perspective to that concept, deepening my understanding of the meaning of sacrifice for another. I experienced first hand what I was learning in Unity Ministerial School—that crucifixion is the sacrifice of the ego and the crossing out of false beliefs. I had been holding onto some old ideas and stories that I needed to release, and somehow the deer woke me up.

Later that week at a prayer class I met a Native American who happened to be from the Deer Clan, and he told me that his people believed that when an animal sacrifices itself in such a way, its purpose is to give you its power. He said that the deer died to give me its "medicine" or healing power of "gentle strength." This has certainly become a necessary remedy in my life work.

The first truth I learned in this experience was that ***the meaning we give to the events in our life is essential***. In other words, whatever story or belief we choose to tell ourselves either empowers us or not. The deer may or may not in fact have sacrificed itself, but the fact that the idea had meaning for me is what counted. It caused me to delve into my own belief system and explore what was working and what needed to be changed. I was able to look for the blessing in the experience rather than to see it merely as an unfortunate accident. It was very timely, since I was about to become a minister and that certainly involves helping others understand the meanings and beliefs that they embrace.

Many people today have a calling to serve in the healing field. Like shamans, these individuals are often "wounded healers." They experience a crisis or a "dark night of the soul," die to an old way of being, and find their way back to health and a more awakened consciousness. Through the ordeal they gain the ability to assist others with their healing as well.

I came to believe that Myrtle Fillmore, cofounder of Unity, was one such wounded healer with a shamanic calling. She was "chosen by the spirits," so to speak, nearly dying from tuberculosis; instead she was healed and then gained the ability to heal others. Charles Fillmore, her husband, followed suit, for he was restored to health and wholeness after a childhood skating accident left him with a shrunken leg and infection causing impaired hearing and vision. But he was more of a dreamer and had many prophetic dreams and visions that guided him in the blossoming of the Unity work.

The Fillmores were role models for me, and the second truth I learned in my experience with the deer confirmed what they had always taught: ***It is important to let go of false beliefs and embrace truth***. Myrtle's healing took place when a lecturer named E.B. Weeks said the words that changed her life, "You are a child of God and therefore you do not inherit sickness." This was a revelation since she had been told all her life that her tuberculosis was genetic. She affirmed that statement throughout each day and spoke words of strength and power to her body, and she was healed within two years. Her husband Charles, followed her example, and was healed as well. Their success gave birth to a prayer circle that became the foundation of the Unity Movement, and it all began with letting go of a false belief and affirming the truth.

The most important belief that I was able to let go of through my encounter with the deer was that I was not worthy to do ministry; I felt that I was not evolved enough or powerful enough or competent enough. All of us experience those inner doubts about our abilities at one time or another. The idea that the deer "died for my sins" was stunning since "sin" is defined in New Thought as "missing the mark of our divine potential." My negative thoughts were preventing me from blossoming and expressing my divine birthright as a child of God with unlimited potential. But I woke up and saw the error of my thinking, and I changed.

The third truth that I learned was that ***all life is sacred***. My devastation at the death of this amazing wild creature felt like

Wake up... Live the Life You Love, In Spirit

a personal loss, especially because it had actually made its way to my car door and looked me in the eye just before it died. Death has a way of putting us in touch with our mortality and the preciousness of life. Suddenly I felt a new reverence for all of creation, a kinship with the planet and all living beings.

Though the experience I have related is out of the ordinary, each of us has moments that wake us up to the realm of Spirit and call us to deeper realization. Next time a significant event occurs in your life, it can be helpful to pause and ask yourself some questions:

1) What is the meaning of my experience?

2) What false or negative belief do I need to let go of and what truth can I replace it with?

3) How does this help me to see that all life is sacred?

When we wake up and take the time to ask and reflect, we discover that spiritual medicine is everywhere.

ფ Rev. Kathy McCall

Conscious Life Design:
Waking Up in the "Hood"
Reverend Bernette Lee Jones

Waking up in the "hood" is not only a spiritual journey, it's
also a trip!

I don't remember the exact day or the specific incident.
Perhaps it was the impact of struggling to survive a series of
inner city ghetto events, like being "put out," a euphemism for
having my belongings set out on the streets of East Baltimore
for not paying the rent. My 3 month old daughter in my arms
stared at me in trust, as the only life support system she knew.
Or maybe it was the time armed robbers came into our West
Baltimore beauty supply store, put a gun in my face, took all
the money and left us on the bathroom floor.

Growing up in the inner city neighbor "hood" gave me a
unique perspective on life. From the "hood" world view, life
was about "do-what-you-can-get-away-with-and-do-it-till-you-
get-enough-to-survive-or-get-caught." In the hood, it seemed
that people just struggled for a living; battling circumstances
was a way of life. Neither the "hard working poor" family values, nor going to the Baptist Church around the corner, ever
woke me up. They seemed to take for granted that, like every-
body else, I merely aspired to be a good struggler when I grew
up.

But something within me yearned for a deeper and higher
truth. Life in the hood could not define or restrain the huge
commitment within me to contribute to the uplift of humanity.
I just needed a bigger God than the one handed down to me.

My soul was calling for a new awareness of God that could
get me through the day to day drama and the mental and

Wake up... Live the Life You Love, In Spirit

emotional struggle that was my companion. I discovered, upon deeper reflection, that the struggles were mostly my desperate fights against depression, anger, rage, and deep-seated resentments for having been incarnated, black, poor, and in such a place as this.

At some point I knew I was being Spiritually guided, although my experiences must have appeared as soap operas to my friends and family. But between the "baby-mamma-drama," and struggling to pay the rent, I was learning to replace old mind patterns and shift my experiences through authentic forgiveness, love, peace and joy.

In my heart there was a vision of helping myself and others to uncover the contributions that we bring to life, even in the hood. I could see the essence of greatness, brilliance and talent within people who struggled to stay out of jail or who fought addictions. It was clear to me they had been incarnated to fulfill extraordinary gifts, but somehow, spent so much time struggling that they never got around to fulfilling them.

I remember one morning, in the inner city park where I walked, I screamed and cried out for help with every ounce of air in my lungs and with all of the soul force I could muster, "God, there must be some way out, because I refuse to accept this way of life any more." I prayed for a way to put my life in some order that made sense of my emerging belief system, the experiences I was having and what I saw in so many others. I shook my finger at God that it was not fair to create people to struggle in the hood. I made it clear that I had no intention of setting foot into another church. My conscious thought was, "OK, God; so if there's something I need to know or do, it'll have to be revealed directly to me." I was startled when it started to happen. More and more, the desire to study and know God for myself in a personal way was all I longed to do. On a daily basis, I was absorbed in God and the search for the meaning of life; often neglecting the necessary things required for routine living, like paying the rent. I had always been taught to believe in God, but realized that I had never believed

Wake up... Live the Life You Love, In Spirit

any of it until the day I realized that God is right where I Am. When I heard the call to ministry, I was frantic and I ran. I just could not understand how God would ever be able to use such a mess to bring a message of hope, freedom, peace, prosperity and possibility to anybody else.

It was a shocking relief to learn that our conscious awareness is our link to God and that our lives are designed out of our own conscious awareness by what we think, say, do and give our attention to in general. I no longer had to be content to let circumstances drive the experiences of my life.

I learned that within my own consciousness is the power to consciously design my life, craft experiences, and say what my life means and stands for. Conscious Life Design emerged as a living system that allowed me to explore the possibility of living from the Christ center of my own being, all of the time. My consciousness of that Truth is the foundation of a principle based way of being and living that flows from the Christ center to shape my personal identity, the family and loving relationships I create, the life work that attracts me, and crafts the community of like minds in which I choose to generate a shared vision. Conscious Life Design is a process we choose to live through. We make intentional, conscious choices, not because something is broken or wrong, but rather, because we love life and have the right to think, choose, be and do by divine authority.

I am now clear that, every experience in the hood and beyond has been for a purpose in the life God has called me to. I am committed to teaching and sharing the possibility to be intentional and in touch with how to have the divine life, the joy filled life of service and generous giving and receiving, flowing abundantly, on purpose, right now. I am committed to Conscious Life Design and I say that waking up in the hood is the perfect place to wake up for those who have chosen to be here. In fact, this time, right now, in the hood, provides a tremendous opportunity for people to wake up.

ღ Rev. Bernette Lee Jones

Wake up... Live the Life You Love, In Spirit

You Came Good Enough
Lola Dowd

I do not believe my story is unique. It merely represents one way a human being decided to "wake up and live the life I love—in spirit."

Part of "waking up" is to let go of the negative ideas and concepts we hold about ourselves. These ideas and concepts bring us pain and prevent us from presenting ourselves to the world as the grandest version of ourselves ever imagined. We have an idea that we need to do something or change something to be more acceptable and happy. (This assumes we are incomplete or unacceptable as we are.) We make the changes, or accomplish the goals, only to find that the search continues. These beliefs about myself, and the resultant pain that this kind of thinking brings, brought me to the miraculous discovery that I need not change anything nor accomplish anything to be acceptable. This search for acceptance is always our search for love. I realized that I was the love I was seeking.

I discovered that I am acceptable in every moment of now. I arrived on this earth for this experience perfectly equipped with everything I need to live a peaceful, joyful, loving life. I learned that this experience is my birthright. I came here good enough.

I gave up my personal history many years ago, when I heard Dr. Wayne Dyer say, "Your past is like the wake of the boat." It is merely the path I leave behind, and its lack of significance is evident when I look back in the water after 5 minutes and realize that it is no longer visible. The only wake visible is the one the boat is making now.

Wake up... Live the Life You Love, In Spirit

The best use of my past is to remember how unwilling I was to be present in it when it was now. I spent many years searching instead of being. This searching assumed that something was missing, something missing in me. It seemed there must be something else out there, or something better must be available.

I came to realize that "seek and you will find" meant "seek and you will be led to the realization that there is nothing to seek." "Ask and it will be given you," came to mean, "ask and you will be reminded that you already have it all." "Knock, and the door will be opened," meant "knock and you'll find the door is already wide open."

For many years I pursued higher education. I felt I wasn't "good enough." I believed that, with the pursuit of each degree, something would be added to me to make me more acceptable. I realized that this path of human endeavor brought me a certificate to hang on the wall and a great deal of stress, frustration, and debt. I didn't realize that I expected the world to respond to these endeavors as something noble and special, and when it didn't happen, I felt rejected.

I began to see the need to "wake up and live the life I loved" when none of my accomplishments changed anything. I decided to embark on my path of spiritual discovery when I was in the third year of my doctoral program. I decided that I was unwilling to obtain yet another certificate, which would hang on my wall, while my life seemed so empty and unfulfilling. I was soon to learn that all those feelings of rejection were simply my judgment of the situation and that they had nothing to do with my "reality."

I became a serious student of spiritual things. I learned to meditate and connect with the "real me"—the spiritual being. I learned to reclaim and accept the real me. I learned that to feel loved, I needed to give love. Sometime later I came to know that I am that which I seek—I am Love. I also came to know that we are all one. We all possess the qualities of the Divine. This allowed me to feel connected to God and to everyone else.

Wake up... Live the Life You Love, In Spirit

I came to know that I wasn't separate from God, and that there was no place that God wasn't. I was able to begin to live the abundant lifestyle I came here to live, with peace, joy, happiness, and contentment. If I wasn't having this experience then I needed to look at things differently, because how I perceive the world is how I experience it. Loving or hostile, I have an opportunity every moment to choose and I choose love. I accepted that everything which comes into my life is for my good and I began to enjoy every moment of the experience instead of letting my life happen while I was searching for what I thought was missing. I found that I have and am everything I want or need. I am the same energy as God, and thus I share all those magnificent qualities—love, patience, kindness, joy, abundance and harmony. All of those things that seemed so difficult to find were there all the time waiting to be rediscovered. I continue to walk this awakened path and continue to learn. When you make the decision to wake up and live the life you love, it is the first step to finding your true self, the spirit you, the real you. If your life seems stressful, unhappy, full of lack, there is hope. Your life can change with a decision for it to change. It will change when you are ready to really know who you are and let go of what you have always believed about yourself, that you are somehow not good enough. You too can wake up and know the Universe is open and ready to assist as you deliberately create the life you love in spirit. You too can come to know that "you came here good enough."

~ Lola Dowd

Wake up... Live the Life You Love, In Spirit

Wake up... Live the Life You Love, In Spirit

How to Live More Authentically by Saying "Yes to Me"
Dr. Janette Marie Freeman

*H*ave you ever stood at the precipice of deep choice, knowing that either choice you make will bring radically different results? Have you ever listened to the voice of Spirit with its passionate cries, seeking to be felt and known, expressed and multiplied in the innermost recesses of your heart's desires? In that moment of choice, did you look out far beyond where you stood, to the possible futures with their joyful promise, or did the needs of others seem so much more important than your own? Will the choice be for Spirit's authentic call of joy and passion, or will the need to please or the fear of disappointing another win out?

There have been so many times when I have thought about making the choice for me, for what I love, but then the struggle sets in. Why is it so hard to choose me? I think about my mother, and my mother's mother, and the mothers before her, and I wonder how many of them had the freedom to choose any portion of a life they loved. Their lives were spent surviving, not thriving. They cared for their children, their husbands, their extended families, and their church communities. Although their service to others was extremely important, there was not much left over for them. Survival was an issue for my ancestor mothers as they carried their children over the plains and mountains into the West. With the beliefs passed down spiritually and physically through the women of my family, is it any wonder that I struggle to give voice to my authentic dreams and yearnings? How could I give voice to big dreams

Wake up... Live the Life You Love, In Spirit

when I was having a hard time asking for what I needed in the simple things?

There are often powerful moments in our lives when we are called to make the choice to say "yes" to our own personal callings. My mother once made a decision for herself, for her sanity and her own Spirit. It wreaked havoc on our family. She left my father to be free of a marriage that crippled her soul. It was very painful for our family. We felt abandoned. The pain lasted for a long time. We children blamed both of our parents. At first we weren't able to see that we would all grow from the experience. I now can admit that my mother's willingness to choose her soul's yearnings taught me a great deal.

Recently I was called to the table of choice. I had been the founding minister of the church in which I was serving. My soul began to yearn for more joy in ministry. Spirit was calling for greater expression, for more creativity and expansion. I made a decision to recreate my personal ministry in a way that honored my soul, my happiness, and my joy. Many in the congregation strongly disagreed with my decision. It pained me, but I know that it was my soul's commitment to greater authenticity calling me to follow the voice of joy.

Why is it so difficult to follow these calls of true authenticity? Is it the old voices in our head that seek to keep us stuck and secure? Spirit's voice continually calls for us to stretch into unknown territory. It is often uncomfortable and it requires absolute commitment to move past the discomfort into the new possibilities.

I am committed to staying connected to the voice of joy, passion, and Spirit as I allow it to lead me and point the way. Living the life I love in Spirit is about waking up to the day-to-day experience of finding Spirit's joy in everyday events and acceptance of what is. I can trust today. It is leading me perfectly; on this I can depend. I know the Life of Spirit is calling me to "choose the authentic me" and that I do not need to judge my choice as selfish or egotistical. The voice of the One

Wake up... Live the Life You Love, In Spirit

that leads me is guiding me to serve the Light more fully, more authentically, and more joyfully.

As I remain committed to choose me, somehow I sense my ancestor mothers cheering me on. My daughters watch me, and I know that they, too, are learning to choose joy's voice.

                  ✍ Dr. Janette Marie Freeman

Wake up... Live the Life You Love, In Spirit

God, the Perfect Travel Agent
Reverend Evelyn Hammond

I had a dream to go somewhere in Europe. Imagine a woman with children having the nerve to have such a dream; the money it would cost. How could it happen? But I chose to dream big. I had been reading inspirational books and I knew that Spirit was always listening, so I prayed and waited. When the trip did not materialize, instead of blaming Spirit I knew I had to do something more, but what?

After more studying, I realized that I needed to move into action. Therefore I devised an Action Plan:

1. I wanted to visualize my trip, so I went to a travel agency and got pamphlets for places all over Europe. I was leaving the destination to Spirit. My faith was growing as I moved into action. Visualize your dream.
2. Next I went to the post office to pick up passport forms. I would need these when the time came to travel. Be prepared.
3. Then I purchased luggage on sale, enough for me and my children. Think big.
4. I was ready to read about Europe, so off to the bookstore I went to buy a travel book. Be knowledgeable.
5. I did some extra work for the purchase of a camera and film. Capture memories.
6. It was time to update everyone's summer clothes; vacation time would be here soon. Dress the part.
7. Next, think about prosperity. I purchased expensive luggage locks. This made me feel rich. Feel wealthy.

Wake up... Live the Life You Love, In Spirit

8. I knew that I would need spending money, so I started buying travelers' checks with no expiration date. This money was earmarked for fun.

9. The pamphlets, passport forms, book, and luggage locks were placed on my dresser so I could see them each day. Keep the dream alive.

Time passed. Our lives were busy. Some friends called and invited me to the Greek festival at their church. My daughter and I attended and had a wonderful time. As we were leaving, one of my friends suggested that we buy raffle tickets for a trip to Greece. After all, someone was going to win. I found just enough change to buy one ticket and dropped the stub in my purse.

Later that evening, my son borrowed my car (he had just gotten his driver's license). The phone rang and my daughter answered. She told me it was a Father on the phone and I immediately thought that my son had an accident. I answered the phone and was asked if I had ever been to Greece! Thank you, Spirit! Prayer works. Wow!

I mailed the papers for our passports, but mine was returned because I didn't have an original birth certificate. Panic set in, as the trip was already set. I called the department that handles birth certificates and the clerk I talked to asked me if there was any way that he could spot my envelope. I told him that my return address is Reseda, California. He told me that he has a sister who lives in Reseda and that he would spot my envelope easily. (That was my second request for a birth certificate.)

We packed, I sent a donation to the Greek Church as a thank you, and off we went—my two teenagers and me. On our flight I met two passengers who asked me whether I was wealthy and I asked them what made them wonder. They told me that it took them years to save for this trip and here I was with two teenagers. I just laughed and told them how I had won the trip. As I walked back to my seat, I realized that I am wealthy, for I have Spirit in my life–the perfect travel agent.

Wake up... Live the Life You Love, In Spirit

We returned home after seeing Greece, where the original Olympics were held, and ending with a cruise around the Greek Islands. It was the trip of a lifetime.

On our way home from the airport as I drove past the Greek Church, the name of the church suddenly registered with me—St. Nicholas Greek Church. Maybe St. Nick is just another name for Spirit. What do you think?

ლ Rev. Evelyn Hammond

Wake up... Live the Life You Love, In Spirit

Wake up... Live the Life You Love, In Spirit

Waking Up Slowly
Dr. Ken Micah Murdock

I have always felt close to God, and although I felt called to serve God in the role of spiritual teacher and minister, I was taught for a long time that as a gay man I was unfit for the priestly role. For years, I lived in fear of exposure, rejection, abuse, and abandonment by friends, family, church, and society. As a result, I became increasingly entrapped in a life spent passing for "straight" in order to survive in a hostile world and serve as a minister.

At first I avoided the growing awakening that I was gay by becoming a monk at age 17, right after high school. Altruistically, I sought to please God, but at the same time I would avoid my real self that I was taught was a condemned spiritual being. There was a constant inner battle between my human consciousness and my spiritual development.

After years of striving to be the best monk I could be, I left the monastery when I realized I was unable to be with those young and wonderful men without desiring a more intimate relationship with them. I am grateful that I never violated my vows when I realized I could no longer stay and be assured I could keep them. In retrospect, I see my monastic life was a gift to help me understand who I am. What I did not yet understand was that God already knew.

Outside of those monastic gates awaited an odyssey that took me from the life of a street person to the superintendent of a school system. I married soon and divorced sooner, looking in vain for that role that would leave me fulfilled yet safely distant from who I am.

Wake up... Live the Life You Love, In Spirit

I married again, this time to a woman I met in a Yoga class. She brought three special gifts to me, our two sons and an introduction to a church where all are welcome. I eventually left the school system to enter the ministry in that church, later moving with my family to pastor a church whose congregation had dwindled to a handful of people.

The church prospered and grew. I was finally free to be a minister, but I had yet to reconcile the issue of my orientation. Over the years, I came to believe life, especially the life of a minister, must be lived in integrity, no matter how painful that may be to achieve. When my youngest son reached adulthood, I separated from his mother amid a flurry of emotions, hoping my faith was leading me in the right direction. Finally, I would be authentically who I am.

Waking up is not always an immediate experience. On some days, we hop out of bed ready to face the day, and on other days, we gradually emerge from sleep somewhere around 3:00 in the afternoon. For me, waking to the realization that I was a perfectly innocent, unconditionally loved child of God who happened to be gay was a lengthy process.

Most of the messages I had heard over the years were that I was unlovable, especially by God. We cannot change the past, but we can change our minds about it. The day came for me to change my mind and believe, instead, that in the beginning I was created in the mind of God as a divine idea, a perfect idea of a spiritual person. What if I were to actually believe that I was a spiritual being living in a spiritual universe, beloved of God, whole, holy, innately perfect, and filled with a capacity for the divine? What would happen if I believed such a message?

What happened is that I am a loved father, grandfather and great grandfather; that I continued to pastor the church that grew and prospered. What happened is I met, and share my life with the man I love, who, like me, is a loving father and grandfather, and I now have become the Dean of my church's ministerial college.

Wake up... Live the Life You Love, In Spirit

Too often we let others put aside our dreams and hopes for the life we would love to live. It is far better to wake up and live it…free in Spirit!

ᥫ᭡ Dr. Ken Micah Murdock

Wake up... Live the Life You Love, In Spirit

"Happily Ever After"
Dyanne Maurer, PhD, DD

"…Happily Ever After" is not a fairytale.
Is it possible? You betcha!

*F*aith is not a fairytale either; it is a dynamic fact. Every experience you'll ever have, everything you'll ever do, everything you'll ever learn will bring you to the next moment. You'd better believe it. Are you focusing upon what you want, not what you don't want? Are you nourishing an element of fear? Fear is the absolute opposite of faith; it is faith in the negative outcome, rather than faith in the positive outcome.

I've married a lot of men in my life. Let me re-phrase that: a lot of men have been married by me. As a "Travellin' Rev" in Las Vegas, I have seen it all. My husband and I have united couples in just about any format you can imagine. That is why the following story was alarming even to my pseudo-sophisticated self.

It was to be a scenic outdoor wedding that would be intimate and romantic, a wedding production that all would find unique. The bride dreamed it would be a day their guests would long remember. Surely she achieved her goal; no one would forget that day!

Half an hour prior to the ceremony, I joined the wedding party to discuss final details. I was told that the ring-bearer was to be a monkey that had been part of the family for over five years. Since I'd seen a variety of critters serve as attendants, I took the news in stride. Though told not to touch, I found the tuxedo-dressed monkey to be a delightful little fellow. The bride confided that she had one real fear: there had been no dress rehearsal with said monkey.

I left the dressing area and donned my floor-length black ministerial robes and collar. It is a very pretty garment for weddings, with very full butterfly sleeves. My husband was the pianist and as he began the musical ceremony on his keyboards, the wedding party came down the aisle. The maid of honor was the bride's daughter. She carried the monkey and preceded the bride. The groom and groomsmen were finely dressed in tuxedos matching that of the pet. The ladies looked lovely, elegantly dressed and with elaborate hairdos piled high upon their heads. It was a pretty picture.

I raised my arms high as I motioned the guests to stand for the bride's entrance. Then all Haiti broke loose. The monkey went crazy, or should I say bananas, and tried to leap from the young maid of honor to the bride. The startled guests reacted with cries of horror while the little monkey screamed back. The girl held on to the leash, but the animal already was airborne while his three-foot tail entangled her hairdo. The chaos had begun. The ring bearer became a bridge between the two gals as his tiny claws wove into their up-dos, which quickly became down-dos. The guests went into shock and all became quiet, except for the little furry monster, who clearly was scared beyond consoling.

My Howard is known for his witty sense of humor, and he truly saved the day. As I prayed for a demonstration of restored harmony, and visualized all things working together for good, Howie began to play and sing, "Abba Dabba Dabba, said the monkey to the chimp."

The crisis was over. Everyone began to laugh as the monkey was carried off and the ceremony resumed more appropriately. The couple later concluded that the monkey thought that my black robes made me into a gorilla. Hmmmmm. The moral here, if there is one, is to wear only sleeveless white when officiating a service involving a monkey!

Do you too find this a fun example of "monkey-see, monkey-do?" Psychologist William James taught: Act as if I am and I will be. This story supports that idea. As in real life, we

Wake up... Live the Life You Love, In Spirit

experience through the law of cause and effect, or as the Good Book suggests, we reap what we sow. What have we put in motion, and what will be its logical outcome? The fact that I can't know God simply by reading about Him doesn't make Him less real. I know God by experience. To receive the gift that has already been given, we must learn to reach out and accept. I can reach out to God in prayer, and so can you.

ɛʌɔ Dyanne Maurer

Wake up... Live the Life You Love, In Spirit

Margaret's Way
Julie Interrante

*I*t's a funny thing when you wear the title of hospice chaplain—people think you know something about God, Spirit, and the big questions of life. It's one of the reasons I've lobbied for a new title for so long, something like "The one who knows nothing but will show up anyway."

Dena, one of my favorite hospice nurses, turned to me one day and said, "We have a new patient who wants to see you. Her name is Margaret. I told her you play the Native American flute. She wants to hear it, but she doesn't want to talk." I said, "Okay," although I did wonder what I was going to do. I always talk with my patients. I agreed, however, to play my flute and keep my mouth shut.

When I arrived, Margaret's son opened the door and ushered me in. Margaret was sitting in an overstuffed rocking chair in the living room. "Hi. My name is Julie. I understand you want to hear the flute," I said. She nodded. The ottoman in front of her became my seat and I began to play. With my eyes closed for focus, I played the melody that was in my heart. After just a few minutes, I heard a faint chirp. I opened my eyes to see Margaret attempting to conceal her tears. I continued to play even though everything in me wanted to ask what she was feeling. I thought to myself, "Dena said, 'don't talk,'" so I obeyed.

When the melody floated away into silence, I put the flute down and took Margaret's hand. Without looking at me, she said through her tears, "I just love music. I admire anyone who can make music—I can't—but I just love music." We sat in silence briefly. I asked if she needed anything more and she

Wake up... Live the Life You Love, In Spirit

said, "No." "It's been a pleasure meeting you," I said. Margaret said goodbye and I left.

I continued to visit weekly and we did exactly the same thing every week for six weeks. I played my flute. Margaret cried, often sobbed. I would hold her hand briefly, say goodbye, and take my leave. There was only one change during those six weeks. Margaret allowed me to hug her after I put my flute away and before I walked out the door.

One afternoon I decided to drop in to see her on my way home. I'd grown very fond of her and wanted to surprise her. When I arrived, her son told me she was in bed. It was the first time she wasn't sitting in her favorite living room chair. When I walked into her room, she smiled and said, "Help me sit up." I did and she sat firmly on the side of the bed. During the next hour, Margaret told her life story. She talked about her childhood, her career and her marriage to the love of her life. She talked about her children, the struggles and the delight of raising them. It seemed at the time and still seems today as though nothing was missed. She shared her fears, her heartaches, and her hopes. She told me how much she appreciated our visits and how the flute touched her soul.

When her story was finished, I helped her lie back on the bed. She asked, "Will you play the flute for me?" I played and she cried. We said goodbye. She asked, "You'll come again next week, right?" "Absolutely," I responded. We shared a hug. "I love you," she said. Kissing her on her cheek, I said, "I love you, too."

Margaret died that night—some time in the early morning hours. My initial reaction was one of sadness and surprise. "She didn't appear to be dying when I was there yesterday," I thought to myself. In the following instant, I knew the timing of her death was perfect. She had done it the way she wanted to do it—with silence and with music. I had done what she requested and then listened to her story when she was ready to tell it. Margaret was a simple woman who died as she lived. She loved music, she cried, she told her story,

Wake up... Live the Life You Love, In Spirit

and when she was ready, she said goodbye and took her leave. Margaret taught me once again the value of putting my own agenda aside and following the wisdom of another soul. Quiet and music created trust. Trust created a safe place to tell the story. Telling the story allowed release and release allowed the beginning of a new story–the divine creative process at work through Margaret and me. I will remember Margaret and her blessing forever.

∽ Julie Interrante

Wake up... Live the Life You Love, In Spirit

Wake up... Live the Life You Love, In Spirit

The Teacher Learns a Lesson
Ruth Wallace

*I*n the midst of teaching a prosperity class I had taught for years, I found myself asking, "Does all this really work? How can I teach this class when I am not feeling prosperous?" At the time, I was ministering in a small church that was faltering financially. I loved the people; they were gracious, caring, and kind, but the church was not prospering.

I had slowly begun to see that my work in this church was to teach the congregation to become leaders. To be spiritually fed, they needed to take responsibility for the direction they wanted their church to go and to define their roles in taking it there.

They had always waited for the *minister* to tell them who they were and what they should be doing. My training told me that their vision had to come from within. That's where they would find their passion. What I didn't foresee was the way in which it would come about.

On April 22, 2004, I happened to watch the "Oprah Winfrey" television show. That day started me on a path that changed my life, and ultimately the life of the church. On the program Oprah was giving awards to several outstanding women. Among them was a woman who had lived on the street as a teenager, when her mother and father had both died of drug overdoses. At the age of sixteen, she decided that it was up to her to change her life, and she did just that.

While watching that show, I realized I felt like a fraud teaching the prosperity class. When I first went into ministry, I made a minimal salary, but my expenses were low and I had excess income. I enjoyed my work so much that I didn't notice

Wake up... Live the Life You Love, In Spirit

something that was creeping up on me. I call it the "stuck in the muck" syndrome. I started shaping my living standards to meet my salary, and I stopped dreaming. I even got into the mindset that ministers shouldn't make much money; they should get paid by the joy of the work! A good friend of mine, Dr. Maria Nemeth, a well-known coach, trainer, and psychologist, once said to me, "I don't know how you ministers do what you do for the money they pay you."

After watching "Oprah" that day, I sat down and wrote out three pages of goals. I realized I wasn't achieving what I wanted to achieve because I had forgotten how to dream. I had been afraid to dream, because I was afraid my dreams were out of reach. That was certainly not an appropriate mindset for a prosperity teacher! I made a pact with myself to live the teachings instead of just mouthing them. I needed to <u>believe</u> that my dreams were possible.

Whenever we commit to something, the Universe obliges us. Six weeks after I wrote my goals, a woman named Sally called to make an appointment with me. That meeting changed my life forever. She told me about a part-time home-based business that involved helping others become healthier and accomplish their dreams. I saw a way to improve my finances and help others at the same time.

The board members of the church where I served were responsible and creative. They had cut the budget to the bare minimum, but expenses still outweighed income. The only expense left was to cut my salary. No one wanted to bring it up, so I took a deep breath, stepped out in faith, and fired myself. It was the right thing to do for the church, and I knew that the Universe would provide for me. The congregation responded by stepping into volunteer positions like never before. We did visioning work to see who they were and where they wanted to go. They took leadership and responsibility for their future.

We found together that our individual lives are a reflection of our inner beliefs. I had believed the myth that ministers

Wake up... Live the Life You Love, In Spirit

don't make much money. They believed that they were not worthy, and that the best ministers would not stay with them for long. By changing our thinking, we both changed our reality. Within a year, my income more than doubled and several even greater opportunities opened up for me. My life is now filled with renewed joy. The church has become financially sound and many of the congregants are taking leadership roles that are bringing new passion into their lives.

The prosperity class? Yes, the teachings do work, but I had to work them. As the Master Teacher said, "All things are possible to those who believe."

cs Ruth Wallace

Wake up... Live the Life You Love, In Spirit

It's Where You Place Your Focus

Denise Yeargin

What was my life like before the wake up call? It was unfocused, or maybe just focused on the wrong things. No one would have known it but me, because most of the people that I associated with were unfocused too. The main purpose of my life at that time was attempting to please others, specifically a God that I thought was somewhere outside myself. But then things slowly began to shift.

It happened almost exactly 20 years ago, which seems like an entire lifetime now. I had grown tired of religion. It wasn't working for me anymore. In fact I had even been kicked out of some religious institutions. I now see that process as a divine order turning point for me, but at the time it felt like the end of my world as I knew it.

As synchronicity would have it, I walked into a Unity Church in Nashville, Tennessee. All I really remember about that day is that I sat on the very back row and attempted to remain hidden. During the place where most churches have prayers, there was a meditation. I had never meditated before so I was a little uneasy, but the minister's voice was so soothing that I was able to relax. At some point during the meditation I began to cry. This crying continued off and on for about a year. The baggage that I had been carrying around inside me was enormous.

I began to spend more and more time in silence, and soon understood why I had been so unfocused for all those years. I had never really been quiet. I had never been taught to listen to that still small voice within whispering to me to wake up. Prayer had been all about me chattering a list of requests to

Wake up... Live the Life You Love, In Spirit

a God outside of me. That same God would in turn answer those requests, only if I was good enough. It took me quite awhile to be able to believe that I was worthy to hear anything God would have to say to me. Soon those beliefs shifted and I began to hear the voice of God.

I remember the day I had the WAKE UP CALL, just like Moses and the burning bush. It was a bright Sunday morning. I had spent time in meditation with God before I woke my two young sons to prepare for church services. On that morning, I heard a message that seemed to come out of a candle flickering on the table. It called my name, "Denise." Well at first I doubted that I had heard anything. But in time as the voice got stronger and stronger, I was able to hear, "Denise, you are the one to bring joy to the world." Joy? How was I to bring joy when my life was so unhappy? My focus had all been about how to fix what I thought was broken in my own life.

I of course asked to see some sort of sign that this message was real. I continued to get ready and fed my two sons. When it was about time for us to leave, I raised the blinds in our living room and looked out into the yard. My oldest son began to speak, "Look Mommy, it's the Easter Bunny." And bigger than life there was a real bunny sitting in the middle of our front yard. At the time, we lived in a very populated area and had never seen anything like that in our neighborhood. I immediately knew that it was my sign. I also heard loud and clear, "Keep your focus on God."

I was a little excited and a little fearful. Who was I to think I could bring joy to the world? I was in a job that I hated and in a place that was literally sucking the life out of me, but as I began to spend more and more time focused on the presence of God in my life, the answers began to come. I had taken on a second job as a part-time Music Minister for a small Unity Church in Nashville. I began to take classes there and to spend more quality time in meditation. I began to have more and more confidence that the messages I was hearing were real. But how was I to bring joy to the world? What did that mean?

Wake up... Live the Life You Love, In Spirit

I realized that I could build confidence in myself if I would be committed to my own spiritual growth. After another year I began to travel to Unity Village in Kansas City, Missouri, to work toward becoming a licensed Unity Teacher. I knew that my calling was toward Ministry but was still unsure how God was intending to use me. One of my instructors there told me that if my dream seemed too big for me, it was definitely mine to do. Her instruction to me was that God wanted me to surrender to the process of creating the life that was mine to have. She also told me that each step would appear when it was time to take it.

Well, four years later, I found myself the Minister of an energetic and alive Unity Ministry called Unity Church for Positive Living, in Donelson, Tennessee. I am not only speaking about how to create a more joyful life, but am also teaching classes about how to have more joy. I am working as a spiritual life coach for several of the members of our awesome congregation as well as for some of the people in our community. My life's work is all about awakening others to the infinite possibilities in this awesome universe in which we live. The life we are meant to live is right in front of us. It is all about the focus. Keep your focus on God!

೧ Denise Yeargin

Wake up... Live the Life You Love, In Spirit

Wake up... Live the Life You Love, In Spirit

Out Of The Cocoon
Carolyn Crane

*I*t was the ending of an old year and the birth of a new one. It was the ending of an old way of life and, as I was to find out, the beginning of a new one. I had given an early morning service for the New Year and had remained to conduct another later in the morning. I finished, walked from the platform, shook hands, shared greetings, and walked the short distance to my office. I remember feeling very tired, unusually so. Then I received a shock that struck me like an earthquake. I started to speak to my secretary and realized that I couldn't formulate a word. For a minister and public speaker, I was in a "heck of a mess." I couldn't talk. I had suffered a cerebral hemorrhage (a stroke) on the left side of my brain.

The emergency room was crowded. It was New Year's Eve. A young man had been shot and was dying. Eventually, I was admitted and was given a very poor prognosis. I was not expected to live, much less have fluent speech again. At that time, I was diabetic, had high blood pressure, and was very overweight. While in a semiconscious state, I was aware of speaking with someone on the "other side." This person was telling me that I would be crossing over and not to be upset when my body was put into a plastic bag and zipped up. The person told me that I would go deeper into sleep and that when I awoke, it would all be taken care of.

Some time later—hours? days?—I regained consciousness and thought, "Hey, I'm not dead. I'm in a hospital room, connected to machines." I could think, conceptually, but I still could not talk.

It had been a stressful year. My husband had been diagnosed with lung cancer the previous winter and had had an operation to remove over half of his lung. It had been a long, slow recuperation. Now, I was ill and unable to communicate. I thought it would be the end of my spiritual career.

I had been a student of various spiritual philosophies for over 26 years and was an ordained minister. Many times I had proven the validity of belief in a higher power and how important a good attitude is toward healing. I thought I had absolute faith in God's greater good to come forth in all things, until I had to face some of these things.

An unusual "miracle" healing occurred shortly thereafter, but I found that even though my speech was restored, my mouth—brain coordination took longer. My memory was faulty and my balance was somewhat precarious.

Five months into recovery, my husband's lung cancer returned. This time it was terminal. This was the bleakest period of my life. I did not know whether I would be permanently impaired or able to continue successfully with my ministry. Also, I had to watch my husband of many years perish with a slow, painful illness.

Then I began to realize that I was being given an opportunity to live the things that I had taught for so long. There is a gift in every problem. One does not have to set things right, one has to see things right. No matter what misfortune may occur, God means all things for good.

Many blessings have come to me since that time. I feel that I am a different person now. I have lost 135 pounds of body weight. When the "weight" was lifted from my soul, it was also lifted from my body. My blood pressure and blood sugar are now normal and I am healthier than I have ever been. One of my goals was to avoid the need to take daily medications and that goal has been met. I no longer need them.

Last year the church where I have been minister and leader for 30 years underwent a transformation. The energy began to change. It has now turned into the Unity Center of Infinite

Wake up... Live the Life You Love, In Spirit

Possibilities. We stress that there are, indeed, infinite possibilities in this life and we are having fun proving this to be true. People tell me that seeing the results of Truth teachings in my life has done more to boost their own faith in good, in God, and in keeping a positive outlook than any verbal lesson I could have given. I came through my "dark night of the soul" with a new vision; with new wings I emerged a butterfly.

ల Carolyn Crane

Wake up... Live the Life You Love, In Spirit

How Much Love Can You Accept?

Rev. Jean A. DeBarbieris

On January 16, 2004, my husband and I became parents for the first time by adopting a beautiful two-year-old girl from Kemerova, Russia. It was the fulfillment of a longing that was decades old and lifetimes deep. I am more grateful for the life of the child who sleeps beside me in her crib than for any other blessing in my life.

Becoming a "late-in-life" parent doesn't lessen the magic of parenthood one iota. In fact, I believe that age allows us to appreciate the wonder of it all so much more than we would have when we were younger. When we are older, life has already taught us that miracles abound and that each one of them deserves to be recognized and celebrated.

So, we daily celebrate the miracle of our child. And, we let her teach us about life. For instance, having been raised in an orphanage for her entire first two years of life, she has several behaviors that are characteristic of children raised in institutions. One of these is the way she self-comforts by "rocking" herself to sleep at night. Watching her, I think it's a lot more "rocky" than it is comforting.

As I lie watching her from my bed inches away from her crib, she engages in her nightly routine. She kicks the bars of her crib and throws her arms and legs through the spaces between the bars over and over again, as though testing the limits of her safety. She sits up, crawls from one end of the crib to the other, pulls the sheets off the mattress, and lies in every conceivable direction and position that is possible to a seemingly boneless toddler. I watch all of this with a mother's heart, and I wish that I could hold her and rock her to sleep

Wake up... Live the Life You Love, In Spirit

in the big, comfortable rocking chair loaned to me for just this purpose.

I long to comfort my daughter and make up for all the tender mothering she didn't have during those first two years of her life. Unaccustomed to being held and rocked to sleep, my daughter doesn't know how to fall blissfully asleep in someone's arms. The most that I can do is give her my index finger to hold. I reach through the bars of the crib, and she responds in kind. Her little hand encircles my finger. She seems grateful for the contact and stops her restless movements. As she falls asleep, her grip relaxes, but she never lets go of my finger completely.

Recently, as we participated in this nightly ritual, I again felt the longing to give her more. I thought to myself, "I have so much love to give her, if only she would let me. I could wrap her in my love by holding and rocking her, but she only wants my finger to hold." Spirit longs to pour Itself completely into us. Suddenly, I realized that this is a universal truth for parents—especially for the Creator, source and sustainer of all life.

Often it's our own sense of unworthiness that hinders the free flow of life, love, prosperity, peace, and all good things that Spirit has already created for us. Over and over again we hear, "It's the Father's good pleasure to give us the kingdom." Who are we to argue with Spirit?

All we have to do is accept! As we become more willing to accept our worthiness as part of God's magnificent creation, we are able to celebrate our oneness together, giving to God the awesome joy and gratitude that naturally follows our inspired awareness that God lives and breathes in, through, and as us!

&⁊ Rev. Jean A. DeBarbieris

"Wake Up…Live *YOUR* Dream in Spirit"

Rev. Rudy A. England

Seven short years ago I had it all. I was a partner in a large law firm. I had a beautiful wife, 2.4 children (well, almost), and a new convertible. I was living on five acres in a home that I had helped design, complete with a backyard pool. The picture of success, I was living the American Dream.

Therein lay the problem: I was living *the American Dream*, not my own. I didn't know it at the time, of course. I had everything I'd ever imagined that I could want. By outward appearances, everything was perfect. But inside I was unhappy—successful, but unfulfilled. My favorite singer, John Mellencamp, wrote a lyric about Americana that metaphorically captures the essence of where I was: "The beds were made, but there were no sheets on."

One Saturday night I walked out of a downtown skyscraper at 10 o'clock. I was supervising a large team of attorneys, working on the largest corporate merger in history. I looked into the nighttime sky and saw a bright, beautiful moon. I realized that this was not it, at least not for me. I was at the pinnacle. Nothing I could do in my career would take me higher. But I had worked 300 hours that month. I couldn't even enjoy my life, not to mention the accoutrements of my success!

My lingering dissatisfaction kept pushing me to search for something more. More "what," I didn't know. I had known that I didn't want to be an attorney all my life, but I just didn't know what else to do. Of course, there were the golden handcuffs that kept me tied to my job—the debt that often comes with the stuff of the American dream.

Wake up... Live the Life You Love, In Spirit

Taking classes at church, it gradually began to dawn on me that there really is something more—an ineffable More that doesn't really care what you call It, only that you awaken to It. Slowly I began to wake up, to recognize the signals, and to see in the events and circumstances of my life that God, Spirit in me, was calling me to be and to do something different.

In one of my classes we were learning to interpret the *Bible* metaphysically, in other words, to find the spiritual meaning rather than the literal interpretation. One evening we were studying the story of the woman at the well in the Gospel of John. After her encounter with Jesus, the woman at the well went back into her village proclaiming to all who would hear, "Come and see a man who told me everything I have ever done!" Though I had found metaphysical interpretation fairly easy to that point, the woman's exclamation had me stumped.

I know now that being stumped can be the precursor to a spiritual breakthrough—and so it was for me. In the middle of the night I awoke with the realization that everything I had ever done in my life had been leading me to become a minister. Christ, the Spirit of God inside of us, is always leading us to our right and perfect place—pushing us to fulfill our own personal dreams, the dreams that God has placed in us. That was what the woman at the well was saying!

Sometimes we have to be told more than once. The golden handcuffs still had me stymied, and a few weeks later, I was at a baseball game telling one of my ministers how dissatisfied I was practicing law. Completely unaware of my earlier realization, his response was, "Have you ever thought about ministry?"

It still took a while. I had to let go of the dream house and overcome the skepticism of family and friends. When you lay everything aside to pursue your own dream, it can be disturbing to those around you as they become aware, consciously or unconsciously, of the latent dreams within them.

Today, as the pioneering minister of a brand new church, I am happier than ever! During the journey I learned that Spirit has a way of providing all we really need, even when we can't see how. We really can have faith that the God who clothes the

Wake up... Live the Life You Love, In Spirit

lilies and feeds the sparrows will care for us when we pursue the dreams He has given us

Today I know I am exactly where I am supposed to be. I don't have the material wealth I once did, but I know there is no substitute for personal fulfillment. I also know that the dreams of others are a cheap substitute for Spirit's unique dream in you! "Seek first the kingdom," and all your true needs and desires will be provided! Wake up…and live your dream; live the life you love…in Spirit!

ॐ Rev. Rudy A. England

Wake up... Live the Life You Love, In Spirit

Wake up... Live the Life You Love, In Spirit

Spiritual Food
Susan EngPoole

Chi fan le mei you – "Have you eaten yet?"

The voice of Spirit called to me at an early age by way of this beloved Chinese greeting. It implies a wish for health and happiness, but more pointedly it addresses the dynamic of human hunger. My parents were passionate about feeding people, and their desire to open a restaurant in the Pacific Northwest in the 1950s opened my eyes, at age four, to the reality of racism. We were the only Chinese family living in the small town of Othello, Washington, and to this day I remember my mother's fear when she learned that a petition was being circulated throughout the community seeking to move our family to a different town.

Several townspeople took a stand to do the right thing, and as a result of their courage and conviction, Othello slowly began awakening to the blessing of cultural diversity. My father and mother, Fred and Jean Eng, opened Freddie's Restaurant, which was consistently featured in the annual publication, *Best Places to Eat in Washington*. For thirty years, my parents served delicious food and tended to the physical hunger of the community that had reached out to embrace them. In all that time, no one was ever turned away because of lack of money, or refused food because the restaurant was closed. If someone showed up between the hours of 3:00 and 5:00 A.M., the only two hours the restaurant wasn't open, Dad or Mom would make the person a sandwich.

Like my parents before me, I have a passion for tending to hunger—the hunger of the human soul. At Unity of Louisville, we serve spiritual food. Each Sunday from the pulpit I offer the assurance that, "Wherever you are on your spiritual journey, you are welcome here." *No one* is turned away.

My direct experience with racism helped shape my passion for inclusiveness, and becoming a Unity minister was a natural out-flowing of my awakening to Oneness with God. Unity of Louisville celebrates the holiness of all people and honors the many paths that lead to God. One Sunday morning, I glanced around the sanctuary and marveled at the fact that we were celebrating Chinese New Year during African Black History Month, in a Jewish synagogue that had been designed after a mid-Eastern mosque. We were more than a concept or a doc-trine—we were a living, breathing portrait of unity.

I was called to Unity of Louisville immediately follow-ing the terrorist attacks of September 11, 2001. I wanted to serve, knowing that prayers, and holding a consciousness of peace, would make a difference. Since the 9/11 tragedy, fear and suspicion have crept into our daily lives. The temptation to give into terrorism mounts with each passing moment, and it's imperative for us to remember that terrorism *cannot* be eliminated by use of force. It will not be vanquished through the erosion of civil rights, or the stripping away of personal freedoms. The secret to its deconstruction lies in the recon-struction of our minds. Scripture encourages us to guard our thoughts—do we have a clear spiritual vision of the peace, wholeness, beauty, joy, and love that surround us?

It is through our communion with God that we're able to recognize and hold fast to the presence of good in our lives. Prayer is the cornerstone of the church. We can move through the world undisturbed by appearances of unrest when we hold to the truth that God is within us. Fear and terror are man-made conditions, and these inharmonious states of mind will vanish when we remember who we are as children of God, one with goodness and love.

Love is the most powerful force in the universe. It isn't something we need to strive to attain—it's who we are. When we understand that we are one with Love, the world around

us will surely reflect our knowing. Our destiny is to create and inhabit the kingdom of Heaven here on Earth.

At Unity of Louisville we affirm that, "There is only one presence and one power in the universe, and in my life: God the Good, Omnipotent." Grounded in this truth, our world is filled with peace, love, joy, wholeness, security, and abundance.

Two thousand years ago, Jesus, our beloved brother and way-shower, extended an invitation for us to come to the table and share in a magnificent feast. Awaken to the truth that you are Love's honored guest at the table of Life.

Chi fan le mei you, my friend—"Have you eaten yet?"

ↁ Susan EngPoole

Wake up... Live the Life You Love, In Spirit

More Than Our Stories
Rev. Trish Hall

*H*ave you ever contemplated: "Who am I?" only to get really confused and perhaps even a bit fearful? For some, it seems the only way to unveil who we are is by wrenching away what we are not. If one has bought into all we've been told and all the interpretations of our experiences that have been thrust upon us by others, the idea of shedding an acquired identity in order to reveal a true self can be terrifying. Often, when asked who we are, we answer a different question: We answer <u>what</u> we are. For instance, I am absolutely confident that I am a spiritual being engaged in a human experience. I am a conscious, deliberate expression of the Divine. That is what I am. Who I am, at the authentic, essential level, is God's highest Divine Idea expressing as me. When we clear away what is unlike that Divine Idea, who we are is made evident by how we appear as an expression of the Divine in the world. *Therefore, you are and I am far, far more than the accumulated stories compiled over the years of being in this human journey.*

The question of *who*, rather than *what* kept haunting me. I tested it on others. Interestingly, most people I asked were stumped by the questions, "Do you know who you are if you cannot use your stories? If you can't whip out your history, how do you identify yourself? What descriptors do you use?"

In our society, we have a propensity for labeling. It is all too easy to paste labels on ourselves: Am I the kid that was too stupid to learn to read, or the child that overcame a learning disability and went on to be successful in business? Am I an adult child of dysfunctional alcoholics? Am I an individual

Wake up... Live the Life You Love, In Spirit

with deep compassion for other victims of violence, or do I wave my status as the survivor of sexual assault as a banner and use it as an explanation for not living up to my potential? Each identifier has a story. We may even expand our identity to fit a story and before we know it, we have embodied it. It may even seem that it has possessed us. The choice is ours.

We may have surrendered our sense of identity to our relationships: I am a wife, a mother, a daughter, a sister, but who am I? When our individuality blurs into our ethnicity or is hidden behind societal labels, our uniqueness gets lost. If we are to reveal who we are, we must reclaim our sense of uniqueness. We are each a unique expression of the Divine—no duplicates! We are more than our ethnicity, our families, and the histories of our families. We are more than our relationships.

Our personal histories and all of our experiences, including all of our dysfunctions and all of our families' dysfunctions, come together into a collage that has helped shape our worldly experience. As long as we are attached to and emotionally invested in those stories, they limit us. The stories define us to the extent that we allow ourselves to be identified by them.

My learning disability was not diagnosed until adulthood, so for much of my childhood, I believed my classmates, teachers, and parents when they said I was too stupid to read. However, at some point I started being resourceful and creative. I would ask a lot of questions of the other students about the reading assignments and then bluff my way through. Many of my teachers didn't even know how little I could read because I could spell. The truth would come out if they insisted that I read aloud. I would have done almost anything to be able to figure out what was on each page. I was a misfit: my classmates could read and I could not. I soon lived up to another label. I became the "problem," I had been told I was.

It's important to look at what compels us to tell our stories. Some of us aren't aware of our innate preciousness. We believe, unconsciously, that if we don't have something bigger or more dramatic than ourselves that we aren't good enough

and we aren't acceptable. Nothing could be farther from the truth. God has consciously and deliberately brought each of us into this life and imbued us with unique gifts and talents *to be shared!* Consider this: Why would God have gone to the bother of creating unique individuals if there wasn't a purpose for uniqueness?

It's time for us to take inventory. What is unique about you? How can you share that uniqueness and with whom? We must learn to appreciate ourselves and our gifts. This may feel awkward for a while, and it is not to be mistaken for egotism. Take a deep, grateful look at yourself and your gifts and talents, the composite that is you, the one that is so much more than the stories. Once we have identified ourselves with how the Divine is expressing in, as, around, through, and throughout us, we discover our authenticity. We open to new ways of being in the world. We find ways to share our unique gifts and talents with others. Suddenly, we no longer "need" to tell our stories.

The compulsion to use stories to describe ourselves is based on a belief that when we stand in our authenticity, naked and unadorned, we are inadequate. This fear chains us to our stories. To break the chains, we need only remember what we are in order to reveal who we are—God's highest Divine Idea expressing as us, uniquely, authentically. The moment that we make the choice to live by faith, knowing that the Life that animates us is the expression of the Divine, our compulsion to tell the stories vanishes. Our need to fit someone else's mold, to create us in alignment with someone else's image of who we are or should be, dissipates and we are free to reveal who we are. We are then innately drawn by our passion for life to live in the world consciously and confidently engaging in selfless service. No longer clouded by our immersion in and dependency on stories to make us acceptable, we can discern the value of our experiences.

Ken Wilber writes in *Integral Psychology,* "Whenever we moderns pause for a moment, and enter the silence, and listen very carefully, the glimmer of our deepest nature begins to

Wake up... Live the Life You Love, In Spirit

shine forth, and we are introduced to the mysteries of the deep, the call of the within, the infinite radiance of a splendor that time and space forgot—we are introduced to the all-pervading Spiritual domain..." Truly, we are so much more than our stories.

        ꙅ Trish Hall

Wake up... Live the Life You Love, In Spirit

The Two Percent Rule

Rev. Robin Haruna

*T*wo percent is not very much at all. It would seem that two percent of just about anything certainly couldn't make much of a difference. Yet by simply changing two percent of the thoughts you think, you can and will change your life.

I remember my first steps tentatively taken on the spiritual path. One of the teachings that really struck me was the concept "Life is consciousness." Consciousness refers to a state of awareness. It might be considered our sense of "knowing." It encompasses our thoughts and feelings. That which we see playing out in our lives is the result of a thought that we feel deeply or of a feeling for which we have a corresponding clear and cognizant thought. When a pattern is formed in the mind, the result will flow forth.

Everything you see in the world around you had its beginnings in the realm of thought. We create our life experience through the thoughts that we hold in consciousness. This spiritual principle is often referred to as the "Law of Mind—Action," or more simply, "thoughts held in mind, produce after their kind." That means that if I don't like my life, **I** have the power to change it and create something wonderful!

But that also means that I am responsible for the messes in my life. So here I am, mucking around in a hole of chaos, confusion, and doubt. Everything just seems so big. How can I possibly move out of this mess and into a state of peace and joy?

Imagine your life as it is today balanced on a pair of scales; this is your "status quo." You can change your life by applying the "two percent rule." Since your life is the result of your

Wake up... Live the Life You Love, In Spirit

thoughts, if you change just two percent of your thoughts, the scales will tip and your life will change.

If you find that your life is in a rut or in state of total chaos, it takes only two percent to tip the scales in one direction or the other. Two percent of your waking time is equal to about 15 minutes. Spend 15 minutes in calm reflection and contemplation, or reading inspirational material, focusing on things that feed your spirit, and your life will change! Likewise, 15 minutes spent in negative thinking or nursing old hurts and resentments will tip the scales in the other direction. Whenever we so much as dip our toes into a consciousness of "inevitability," that which our heart desires does indeed come into our lives. It simply cannot be otherwise. So where do we begin?

We must first believe that a certain something is possible. We must affirm the willingness and open-mindedness to conceive the possibility of that which we desire. Do you really believe that it is possible for you to live a life of fulfillment and joy? If not, that is where you must begin to place your two percent of thought. Remind yourself that it is possible to find more satisfaction in your daily life; picture yourself content; visualize those things that bring you joy. Focus on this possibility for a mere 15 minutes each day.

As the scales tip, move from possibility into the realm of probability. Begin to think and feel that, "Yes! I probably could live a life of joy, freedom, and satisfaction. I probably could see that manifest in my life." Move from the notion that something just might be possible to the idea that it is indeed probable.

Now comes the moment in which you switch into *inevitability.* Over time, you have come to truly know not only that your good is possible, but that it is probable. As your capacity to believe and receive the goodness of the Universe increases, your thoughts continue to tip the scales, bit by bit, two percent, 15 minutes. The delicate balance between probable and inevitable, tips completely and totally into the realm of manifestation. Hold to the idea of what you desire in your life

Wake up... Live the Life You Love, In Spirit

in your mind and heart—your thoughts, your feelings. That which you have conceived becomes inevitable. The good that you desire cannot help but appear in your life.

I have witnessed the result of this concept time and time again in my personal life. The very moment at which I switch into the consciousness of inevitability, Boom! There it is! That which I have desired, from a loving, fulfilling relationship to a beautiful place to live, is now present in my life. It began with simply changing two percent of my waking thoughts, a mere 15 minutes engaged in a more positive and focused vision of what I wanted to experience in my life. Two percent—it seems like such a little thing, but it will change your life.

℃ Rev. Robin Haruna

Wake up... Live the Life You Love, In Spirit

Perfectly Ordinary
Margee Grounds

Scientist Fritjof Capra wrote, "Doing work which has to be done over and over again helps us recognize the natural cycles of growth and decay, or birth and death, and thus become aware of the dynamic order of the universe. Ordinary work, as the root meaning of the term 'ordinary' indicates, is work that is in harmony with the order we perceive in the natural environment."

Usually we humans don't place much value in the ordinary. Yet when extraordinary times come, we repent—which simply means "to think again" (change our thinking or outlook or perspective). I learned this truth during an extraordinary time in the life of my sister, Dorothy. I was talking with her on the telephone while she was lying on her sofa, incapacitated with terminal cancer. She was alone in the house because her husband was off to his ordinary work day, and her sons were in distant cities living their ordinary lives, and I was at my office on an ordinary weekday.

Dotty said, "If only I were well enough to go to work!" She longed for an ordinary day. This brought me up short because I was wishing for a day that was NOT a work day—a day off. It made me realize that I really needed to be mindful of what I wished. I could get what I wished for and find that it wasn't what I wanted at all.

Recognizing this truth did not make me change completely. Yes, I have learned to appreciate having the ability to work and I have come to understand that doing my work is a privilege. It is an honor to contribute that which I can do well, that which is mine to do, and that which is needed. But ordinary, rou-

Wake up... Live the Life You Love, In Spirit

tine work such as dusting, laundry, and cooking is difficult to appreciate. All too soon it is time to start these types of tasks again.

Not until I read the Capra quotation did I realize that work which has to be done over and over again is capable of teaching me something important. I like things to be done once and for all. What an illusion that idea perpetuates! Suppose I could do something and it would never have to be done again? Suppose I did it wrong and, because the "doing" was permanent, I could never do it better? Because things need doing over and over again, second chances (and thousandth chances) are possible!

I can't say that I'm cured yet, but I do realize that I have a resistance to routine tasks. That's the first step, isn't it—awareness? My prayer for those of you who read this is that you can move further up the ladder of awareness. Perhaps your progress will pull me along. I believe that God uses group consciousness to help all of us to progress. We are like mountain climbers tethered together. When one of us loses his or her footing, the others hold fast, until the fallen one regains position. Then we progress again, until another one gets careless or weak or just simply makes an error.

ↄ Margee Grounds

Wake up... Live the Life You Love, In Spirit

My Father's Life and Death Legacy
Peggie O'Neill

"I tried to teach my children how to live; now I'll try to teach them how to die." —J. Eustace Wolfington, Nov. 1955

*M*y father, J. Eustace Wolfington, was a rainmaker. The ultimate teacher, he transformed small life events into large character-building lessons. Dinnertime was learning time. He started with a prayer before engaging us in lively conversations or debates on people, faith, business, politics, sports, and school. He held our attention with stories about God, family, business, and ordinary and extraordinary people. He ended most dinners with quizzes on what we discussed at dinner or quizzes on current events. With a twinkle in his eyes and a smile on his face he'd put a dollar bill on the table and ask us a final question that challenged us to think. The winner got the dollar.

He taught us to be self-sufficient and to earn our own money working after school and during the summer. He encouraged us to give 10% of our time and our earnings to charity. He purchased a small summer hotel and restaurant on the beach for us to run. Mother was the president; we were the board of directors. We marketed it, managed it, and worked it. He adored and respected my mother and he taught us to do the same. I can remember many nights when he and mother stayed up half the night helping me resolve some painful teenage issue. He had a magical way of helping us take responsibility for and solve our own problems.

We never considered that our energetic dynamic father would die, until that fateful day in November 1955, when he was diagnosed with terminal lung cancer. He was 48 years old. When he heard the prognosis he and mother held each other

Wake up... Live the Life You Love, In Spirit

and cried. Then he wiped his eyes and declared, "M.M., we taught our children how to live; now we can teach them how to die."

He had a mission, the most important and final mission of his life. He wanted to teach his nine children how to die and he didn't have much time. Although the cancer spread to his stomach, making him very ill, he refused pain-killing medicine. He wanted to be mentally sharp. He planned a private one-on-one conversation with each of us. He was growing weaker by the day and he knew his time was running out.

He told us he wanted us to remember him in his hospital bed where he didn't even own the gown on his back. "The only thing that matters now is my relationship with God, my relationship with your mother and you children, and my relationship with my fellow man." He explained, "Some day you will be here and the only thing that will matter for you will be your relationship with God, your relationship with your family, and your relationship with your fellow man. As you go through life there will be times when you will be tempted to compromise these relationships for worldly gain. When those moments come, I want you to remember me in this hospital bed and remember what's really important. If you measure your actions with God, your family, and your fellow man, you will make the world a better place to live for all people. And you will have the same peace I have when you come to this sacred place where I am now."

He told us that he loved us and he was proud of us. He told us he wanted mother to remarry. "Your mother is young. The living must go on with the living. If we believe what we claim to believe I will be rejoicing in heaven and your mother should be enjoying a full life on earth." He put an addendum in his will that mother should remarry. He laughed and assured us mother would marry someone wonderful. "The men will be breaking the doors down when I'm gone."

He died the day after Thanksgiving, November 25, 1955, with mother and his children around his hospital bed. He

Wake up... Live the Life You Love, In Spirit

spoke to us right up to the last minute. He was physically frail, but spiritually strong. He told us not to cry, he said, "I'm very tired; let's just pray." He turned his head and said, "My Jesus mercy," and he was dead. Although he died fifty years ago, his legacy lives on in the hearts of his nine children, sixty-eight grandchildren, one hundred great-grandchildren, and the many foundations and charities started by his children and grand-children. But the greatest of his legacies is his living example of the road he traveled to "this sacred place." The only thing that matters is your relationship to God, your family, and your fel-low man. Remember that, and the world will be "a better place for all people."

                                       ❧ Peggie O'Neill

Wake up... Live the Life You Love, In Spirit

Wake up... Live the Life You Love, In Spirit

The Prescott Baby
Georgia Prescott

I used to think God wasn't paying attention when, as I was riding to my mother's womb on the conveyor belt headed for California delivery rooms, I was issued a body which refused to bend into yoga positions, and given a copy of the *Sporting Green* instead of my own journal and a pastel pencil set that all of the other California babies were issued.

Then I joined the Santa Rosa Church of Religious Science and found out that God is always paying attention and never makes mistakes, so I decided that maybe I was part of a control group. I could vaguely hear Peter saying to Gabriel, "Let's give the Prescott baby a short round body, the most critical mother and the most absent father in all the land, and the Lesbian gene. Then let's check in on her from time to time and see how she does."

And they did. They were there watching, and maybe praying, when I was 11 and being stuffed into the dress with all the ruffles for my Confirmation. They heard me trying to tell Mrs. Prescott how the dress didn't feel right. Mrs. Prescott thought it was because the material was scratchy, not the Lesbian gene, so she told me she wouldn't use starch next time. Watching and praying were not very effective.

Surely they were there when I was 17 and fell in love for the first time with another Catholic Daughter of The Golden West. They saw the shy glances, the tongue-tied conversations, the awkward first kiss. Unfortunately my sweetheart's mother saw the second kiss. She called Mr. and Mrs. Prescott and told them their daughter was unnatural. I could hear Gabriel tell Peter that the Lesbian gene must be very powerful. It's the first

Wake up... Live the Life You Love, In Spirit

time Mr. Prescott has ever cried. He came back pretty quick, though. All three of us got in their 1954 Dodge and drove to the parish for a conference with Sister Timothy. We arrived in shame and left in shame because nobody knows how to talk about the Lesbian gene. On the way home, Mrs. Prescott mentioned how she wished the baby had been born to someone else. I decided right then that watching and praying wasn't worth much.

I didn't hear much from Peter or Gabriel until I heard one of them (I'm not sure which) say to the other, "the Prescott baby had her 30th birthday not long ago, let's see what's what. Why is she sitting there in that circle with everyone who has such shaky hands and red eyeballs? And why is Jesus there masquerading as a heterosexual man in a baseball cap saying, 'only rigorous honesty in all our affairs yields us freedom from alcohol?' Why is the Prescott baby crying? Maybe we should have done something." Yes, boys, you should have. But I'm not sure what.

It wasn't long after that I was trying to get someone to notice me who I'd heard was singing in the Santa Rosa Church of Religious Science choir. I ironed my best flannel shirt and sat in the first row so that I might be noticed in a devout posture. I was truthfully a little nervous that Sister Timothy might march down the isle and snatch me up by my ear, being in a God-knows-what-kind-of-church.

Then this lady minister, her name was Rev. Mary Murray Shelton, came out and said something no one had ever said to me before. She said that I was whole, perfect, and complete just as I was. I'm sure she said other things after that, and I'm sure the choir sang their songs but I didn't hear any of it. I'd be surprised if anyone around me heard anything either because of the torrent of sobs coming from deep somewhere inside of me. Deep cleansing sobs that said, "You're home. You can let go of the shame you think you caused your parents; you can let go of your resentment of Gabriel and Peter. They could only be with you, not do for you. You're

Wake up... Live the Life You Love, In Spirit

welcome here, really welcome. Not in spite of who you are but in light of who you are."

I only overheard Peter and Gabriel one more time. It was at my ordination as a Religious Science Minister in a church I founded in Sacramento. I heard one of them, I'm not sure who, say to the other, "Well, look at the Prescott baby, she's attracted a very diverse group of people who are ready to hear they're whole, perfect, and complete." I think I heard a little pride in his voice. I hope he told Mr. and Mrs. Prescott. They're up there with them somewhere. I think.

ᐇ Georgia Prescott

Wake up... Live the Life You Love, In Spirit

Wake up... Live the Life You Love, In Spirit

Intent
Gregory Scott Reid

Over the past few months, things in my life have been better than ever—new home, new friends, and a wonderful career. Yet I found myself uncharacteristically asking, "Self, why am I feeling so frustrated? Why am I getting upset at the smallest of situations?" I did a little digging (soul searching, if you will) and realized that as wonderful as things were going at the moment, like most of us, I had some unfinished business out there. There were a handful of people and negative relationships that were still on my mind and I wanted to do something about it.

What I came up with was this realization: of all the people or things I was angry with, none of them truly meant to cause me harm. In other words, they had no malicious intent. It was only my interpretation of the event or situation that caused me anger and pain. How many times have you gotten into arguments over the silliest of things, only later to realize how foolish you were being and acknowledged that you had simply gotten caught up in the moment?

After pondering this question, I decided to do something I should have done long ago. I thought about the few relationships in my life that were less than perfect or that had ended on a sour note. I then committed myself to research what had caused the upheaval and to do my best to rectify the relationships that lacked a harmful intent.

I asked myself whether my ex-wife had really intended to slander me with the things she said, or whether she'd been speaking through her frustration and uncertainty of losing a relationship that she had shared for over half her lifetime. Had

Wake up... Live the Life You Love, In Spirit

my father intended to discard our relationship, or was he simply avoiding me to save himself from having to deal with his own ex-wife, who may have said some terrible things to him as well?

As personal as this is, I share it with you because what happened next was truly amazing. By taking action to repair the past and eliminate the negative feelings I was carrying, I rekindled some of the best relationships I'd ever known.

We cannot know what other people are thinking. However, we can turn to God and look within, using some good old-fashioned common sense to make an educated guess. For example, if someone borrows your car and crashes it, you should ask yourself whether they meant to do it. Of course, they didn't, so why end a relationship over it? However, if someone takes a bat to your car and smashes it to pieces, you're safe in assuming they had a negative intent.

Do you have any relationships that may have been severed because of an accident or a misunderstanding? In retrospect, do you think the person truly intended to distress, upset, or provoke you? Was a baseball bat involved, or just angry words and misguided thoughts? If you can't find evidence of a harmful intent, pick up the phone, say hello, and let go of your resentment.

Best wishes and, whatever you do, keep smilin'.

ల Gregory Scott Reid

...And I Stood There Staring into My Son's Dead Eyes
Donald Peters

I never used to think too much of prayer. In fact, even though I practiced it at church, I had always been skeptical about the actual power of prayer. My belief was that prayers were said in church and, in the case of my children, just before bedtime. I believed that it was a tool to bless people and sometimes to ask for forgiveness. I never believed that if you prayed for something for yourself that the prayer would be answered. Up until the event I am about to relate to you, I was an occasional church-goer—Christmas and Easter. I only went because we would spend that time with family and Mom always made us go, out of guilt if nothing else. Then one day, everything in my life changed. It is sad that it took a tragedy to awaken my spirituality.

One May weekend we were visiting my in-laws in central Texas. My wife, Julie, had given birth to our daughter, Kaylin, only a few weeks earlier. Our son, Jonathan, was two-and-a-half years old. We had just left New Jersey after I had been laid off from a computer project manager position. I was in the back office of the house sending out resumes, trying to find work. Suddenly Julie's dad ran in and said, "Don! Jonathan fell into the pool!" When I looked into his eyes and saw terror, I knew that something was wrong. I jumped out of my chair and ran out the back door. As I looked across the pool, I could see my mother-in-law standing, looking down, and crying. Julie was on her knees over Jonathan, who was laid out on his back and she was giving him mouth-to-mouth resuscitation.

Wake up... Live the Life You Love, In Spirit

I got down on my knees and looked at my son. His eyes were wide open, and he was turning blue. He was dead, there was no breath. His eyes had that dead blank stare. I grabbed his limp, cold leg and begged him to breathe. I was also praying, "Oh God, please, make my son breathe." But Jonathan remained motionless. I began to rub his belly and told him, "Breathe, Jonathan, breathe. We want you to live!" I yelled for my father-in-law to call 9-1-1.

Julie continued with mouth-to-mouth. I was crying and begging Jonathan to breathe. Minutes passed and I was terrified. I was thinking, "Oh, my God, my son's dead."

All of a sudden, a little spurt of water came out of his mouth, and he made a choking sound. Was it an after death reflex? Then he started to gasp, and then nothing for a minute or two. He was breathing erratically, but I could see some color coming back into his lips. At that point I began to have hope. At about that time, the ambulance came, and the paramedics took over. They put a bag over his mouth and began to work on him. I was shaking, shocked over what was happening. When I saw that he was breathing, I began to feel a little relieved, and I said out loud, "Thank you, thank you, thank you."

Julie went in the ambulance and I followed in my truck. Jonathan was taken to the emergency room and they directed Julie and I to an office to fill out paperwork. For the first time, Julie began to cry. "Don, I'm so sorry; I thought Mom was watching him, and she thought I was watching him. I didn't mean to do this; I am so sorry," she cried. I hugged her and I said, "It's not your fault. Don't worry about it, he going to make it; he's doing fine and he's going to be great. It's all going to work out."

Finally we were allowed to enter the emergency room. Before we went in I was expecting Jonathan to be up and peppy and laughing. When I saw him I was shocked. His fingers were locked together in tight twisted fists, his arms were splayed, and he was screaming. The nurse could not answer

Wake up... Live the Life You Love, In Spirit

any of my questions about his condition and if it was permanent or not. Here was my little genius, reduced to a child that could only grunt, moan and scream.

Jonathan stayed like that for hours. During that time, I got on my knees next to his bed and prayed a prayer of desperation. "God, please, bring my son back to me; I will do anything. I will go to church every Sunday; I will be a faithful servant. He is the innocent one; I should be the one punished, not him. Please let him live and be the little boy that he was, that we remember. Help him through this; help me through this." It was probably the first time in my life that I actually asked something of God and really had to believe that he would answer my prayer.

I had to get out of the emergency room for a while to gather my thoughts. I went outside and decided to call my father to update the family on Jonathan's progress. My dad told me that my mom (a typical Italian Catholic mother, crosses and religious artifacts throughout the house) had started a prayer chain. Prayers were going throughout the country right at this moment, praying for Jonathan's recovery. At that moment, I did not much think of the prayer chain. I had already given my own prayer. I stood there, fully doubting that anything positive could happen.

At some point in the evening they transferred Jonathan to pediatric intensive care at another hospital, one that was better equipped to handle pediatric emergencies. Julie and I took positions near Jonathan's bedside. He had been asleep since our arrival and the nurse had nothing to tell us except that he needed his rest. Julie and I spent many of the past eight or so hours holding and reassuring each other, silently praying for a miracle. At about three o'clock in the morning, something wonderful happened. Jonathan suddenly popped up and said, "I'm thirsty." Just like that. We both began to hug and kiss him. His speech was normal, and he was acting the way I remembered him. Amazingly, Jonathan was discharged the next morning, and later that day was running around the house as if

Wake up... Live the Life You Love, In Spirit

nothing happened. Although Julie and I were totally exhausted, we were full of exhilaration and relief.

I fully believe that Jonathan's recovery was a miracle. I no longer question the power of prayer. I take the time to pray for others as needed, something I never did in the past. I know that prayer works, that God listens, and that I need not be ashamed to ask for help with my dreams. I will never be afraid to ask, to question, and to hope. I hope that you will do the same. God is very generous and giving and He just may fulfill your wishes.

಄ Donald L. Peters

Wake up... Live the Life You Love, In Spirit

Power of Affirmations
Dr. Anne Marie Evers

"*I*n the Beginning was the Word, and the Word was with God, and the Word was God" (John 1:1). King Solomon acknowledged the power of the Word when he said, "As a man thinketh in his heart, so is he." Today we call the power of the Word "Affirmations."

Today with the added stress of society, people from all walks of life are discovering the power of affirmations to set their goals and make them happen. Some of the stories I receive through my website and in the mail are simply amazing. They carry a strong message that there is much more than affirmations happening when you engage in these methods.

Affirmations are a magical tool to assist you when you are going through difficult times and give you the assurance things will work out for you. Affirmations also assist you in attracting happy relationships, abundant health, prosperity and much more!

Affirmations are similar to prayers, wishes, or goals; only they are more structured and specific. To affirm is to make firm. The basis of all affirmations is positive thinking.

The following is the core of the methods I've used to help 1000's of people achieve success. I have many more in my other books than the ones I have included here, but this is a good start to learn about the power of affirmations.

The Four Cornerstone Affirmation Program

1st Cornerstone: Forgiveness

Forgiveness is very powerful and it can heal even the deepest wounds. Forgiveness is the process of untangling mental and emotional parts of our being. Forgiving is a choice–as is

Wake up... Live the Life You Love, In Spirit

not forgiving. Forgiveness has powerful healing properties: it reduces stress, lowers blood pressure, and increases well-being. It can also reduce the risk of cancer and other disease.

2nd Cornerstone: The Power of Thoughts and Mind Power

(a)   Thoughts

What is the greatest power that has ever been discovered? The power of wealth or fame? I believe it is the power of your thoughts, mind and imagination. Thought is creative and it is the first and most crucial stage in the development of any new idea, business, or other venture that becomes reality. Having thoughts actually create new brain cells and causes physical and chemical changes in your brain. Through thought your mind can be programmed at will, and reprogrammed as frequently as required. As the most powerful and reformative tool at our disposal, thought must be used wisely if we are to create what we want out of life.

(b)   Mind Power

We have one mind, with two distinct, yet interrelated, functional characteristics. One is the conscious, objective, waking state. The other is the subconscious, subjective or sleeping state. The subconscious mind is a part of God's Mind, which is all powerful, all knowing.

3rd Cornerstone: The Power of Affirmations

If you ever blew out the candles on your birthday cake and made a wish, you have done an Affirmation. You are here to evolve and grow. You are a co-creator with God, with absolute control over your thoughts and words and therefore yourself. Using the tremendous power of your mind and properly worded Affirmations, you can become a magnificent creator and a magnet for all your desires.

Any Affirmation declared with commitment and belief manifests that which it affirms. All Affirmations must be done to the good of all parties concerned, and this includes you.

4th Cornerstone: Creative Visualization

This involves using your imagination to create the manifestation of your desire. It is a natural power that we all possess

Wake up... Live the Life You Love, In Spirit

whether we are aware of it or not. Your mind does not know the difference between a real and an imagined event. Thinking in pictures is one of the basic activities of the human mind. When you desire positive changes in your life, use vivid, mental images to create the experience you desire.

Making Your Affirmations Effective

Affirmation Garden –Four Step Process

Step 1: Soil Preparation and Seed Selection. Prepare the soil of your subconscious mind by forgiving everyone or everything that has ever hurt you. Now the freshly, prepared soil of your subconscious mind is ready to receive the seed.

Step 2: Plant the Seed (Your Master Affirmation). Decide what you want, being very specific so that your affirmation is tailored to suit your individual needs and desires.

Step 3: Water and Fertilize. Read your Master Affirmation every morning and evening, knowing that your subconscious mind is always listening, taking in every detail and storing it for all time.

Step 4: Anticipate the Harvest. Mentally step ahead 3-4 weeks or months and creatively visualize yourself obtaining your goal. Engage the five physical senses.

You already have the manifestation of your desire;
it simply has not yet appeared in your reality as yet.

Your Sample Master Affirmation
<u>Note:</u> *Use words that trigger feeling and emotion in your body.*

"I, (your name), deserve and now have or am:

_____
(Write your desires.)

to the good of all parties concerned. Thank you, thank you, thank you."
I fully accept.
Signed: _____ Dated:

When you have signed and dated your Master Affirmation, you have made a firm and binding contract with your Higher Self, God, Creator.

Make your Master Affirmation colorful because color wakes up and excites the subconscious mind.

Master Affirmation Checklist
- Is it specific? Does it contain the 3 P's—personal, positive and present tense?
- Did you release negativity?
- Are your heart and mind in agreement with your Affirmation?
- Is it to the good of all parties concerned?
- Is it designed not to hurt or take from anyone?
- Is there at least a 51% believability factor that the Affirmation can manifest?

If you answered *Yes* to all the above questions, congratulations! You have just completed your first Master Affirmation!

Teach Affirmations to Your Children

Teaching your children to use the power of positive Affirmations at a young age is one of the best gifts you can ever give them. Say Affirmations directly to children. A child's inner talk does not just happen. It is born of what children hear from other people. They absorb words, feelings, actions, and beliefs from you and others and they internalize them. Be consciously aware of the words you use when interacting with your children.

Affirmation Success Stories
One Kid's Review: "This Book Rocks!"

I am so lucky my mom gave me a copy of your book on Affirmations to read because I know most people my age don't know about Affirmations.

Before I read your book, I used to keep my feelings inside me. But now I know how to express them. I think they should have this book in all schools and libraries in the world! I also want to thank you for helping me and showing me the way to change my life to live more positively.

Adrian, Grade 7 North Vancouver, BC Canada

From Living on the Streets of Vancouver to a Loving, Happy Home

James Harvey was a homeless young man living on the streets of Vancouver when he started reading my book,

Wake up... Live the Life You Love, In Spirit

Affirmations Your Passport to Happiness. He memorized the Short Form Affirmations and put them to music. He listened to them over and over. Then miracles began taking place in his life. He manifested a fantastic place to live, musical equipment, clothes, computer, and other things. He called to tell me of the wonderful things taking place in his life after doing Affirmations and asked me how he could give back to God. I suggested that he put together a positive musical CD for my anti-violence Children's Program, *The Affirm and Learn Enhancement Program* and he did! I am so proud of him!

Creating a Hospice Using the Power of the Word and *The Affirmation Magic Magnetic Circle Method*:

For many years, the Crossroads Hospice Society held the vision of having our own free-standing hospice. We knew that Affirmations when properly done would produce results. From magazines, Anne Marie and I fashioned a circle of pictures for our Hospice scrapbook, showing the desired colors and the homelike environment we wanted to achieve in the hospice. We wrote the names of the corporations, foundations, and community leaders we wanted to contact and added the positive words that would create the Affirmation Magic Magnetic Circle.

Over the course of four years, the Affirmation Magic Circle enlarged. With the efforts of many dedicated community citizens and our Capital Campaign Chair Tracy Price, we were able to raise the funds to build our free-standing hospice. Thank you, Anne Marie. You were the catalyst that enabled us to fulfill our dreams. *Linda Kozina, Hospice Manager Crossroads Inlet Centre Hospice.*

"Anne Marie has provided a comprehensive easy-to-follow system for transforming destructive or limiting core beliefs. Her books help put you in charge of your programming and, consequently, in control of your life!" *Lee Pulos, PhD.*

Affirmations Are for Everyone!

This reader writes, "I am a 36-year-old male who has been in prison for 16 years. I have your Affirmations book about accessing the power within and the method of doing

Wake up... Live the Life You Love, In Spirit

Affirmations. I found it very interesting and informative. When I started reading, I was very angry and then I discovered I needed to forgive. I started on this forgiveness process. I have been doing Affirmations for justice in my case. It was recently reviewed with favorable results! Thank you, Miss Evers, for being a part of my long, rocky, but wonderful journey of healing! *Name of person and prison withheld.*

Realtor Merv Wright writes, "As a result of reading your book, I started doing Affirmations on a daily basis—to my benefit. I used your method to create both personal and business changes in my life and I received positive benefits and results. I even take your Affirmations book to church and often find similar and confirming information in the sermons. I use this combined information to create an uplifting, positive environment in my life. It works!!! Recently I had a challenging business situation. A difficult seller refused to make a price adjustment to bring the selling price of his home into line with other homes. I wrote a Master Affirmation that my listing was now sold for the perfect price. I placed a picture of the house at the top of the Affirmation and wrote SOLD across the photo in large red letters. Well, that process worked!!! To my delight we received an acceptable offer within 10 days. W-O-W: Affirmation Selling Success!" *Do affirmations work? You bet they do!*

From Chaos and Unhappiness to Love, Happiness and Abundance, Affirmations has helped me in many aspects of my life.

- Affirmed for a quick sale of my house for the asking price and it sold within three weeks—*above* the asking price.
- Affirmed "Big Money to me Now". I retired with more money than expected and was even able to pay off the loan on my brand new car.
- Received a large sum of money from an unexpected inheritance.
- Affirmed for the perfect man for me for a loving, lasting, happy relationship and I met the *man of my dreams on a cruise.* We are now engaged to be married.

Wake up... Live the Life You Love, In Spirit

Yes, Affirmations do work! You just have to be very clear about what you are affirming. (or ordering up). *Darlene Jensen, Coquitlam, BC, Canada.*

My Own Story of Disbelief to Belief!

For many years I have used Affirmations in all aspects of my life with wonderful, sometimes startling results. When my husband Roy became suddenly ill, I started doing an Affirmation that he get well. I did it regularly with faith and expectancy and—*he died!*

I was devastated and started doubting the whole process. Then I heard a little voice in my head say, "What would you tell others?" It kept on so I finally said, "I'd tell them there is hope." Then instead of stopping, the little voice in my head continued." Why don't you notify yourself?" So I did. I now know my Affirmation did work! I rationalized it this way. I am not God; I cannot say how long people live. I was the one doing the affirmation—*not* Roy. I realized it was his time to go. I also took strength from the Serenity Prayer. I believe Roy is back at Source with God where he *is* 100% healthy. I believe my strong Affirmations empowered him with strength to cross over.

As for me, since Roy's passing three years ago, I have completed my ministerial studies and am an ordained Minster. In July of 2005, I received my Doctor of Divinity. I have written four more books on the power of Affirmations and created two Children's Program for the prevention of violence. My faith in God and the power of His Word in Affirmations is even stronger!

And I know that, Affirmations When Properly Done Always Work!

℘ Dr. Anne Marie Evers

Wake up... Live the Life You Love, In Spirit

Author Index

Jim Chandler's vision was of a Church founded on a belief in empowering its congregation and the great community it serves. This vision became a reality in 1997 as The Denver Church of Religious Science where he serves as Senior Minister.

The Church serves as a resource by supporting and serving numerous other non-profit service organizations throughout Denver. Reverend Jim's commitment to service in his community goes beyond the Church. He has been appointed by the Mayor of Denver to serve on the Mayor's Advisory Council on HIV/AIDS. He has been a member of the Planning Committee which creates and organizes the annual Denver Martin Luther King Day celebration, one of the largest celebrations in the nation. He regularly serves on the Board of Trustees and Advisory Committees for other non-profit organizations. He was most recently appointed the Ecclesiastical Representative for the United Church of Religious Science as the local representative serving over two dozen Religious Science Churches throughout the Rocky Mountain and Plain States, as well as his regular duties as a member of the teaching faculty of the Denver Campus of Holmes Institute. He is continually finding ways to serve others in creative and empowering new ways.

Website: DenverChurchofReligiousScience.org

The Chopra Center for Well Being
7630 Fay Avenue
La Jolla, CA 92037
Fax: (858) 551-9570

Wake up... Live the Life You Love, In Spirit

Internationally acclaimed inspirational and motivational speaker, counselor to the "Stars," & best-selling author of 6 books including *What You Think of Me is None of My Business & Dare to Be Great*. Her weekly, international, Emmy winning TV program inspired millions. Featured on over 800 TV and Radio shows including *Oprah* and *Larry King*, featured in *People, US, Newsweek, Time*, the cover story of *The Wall Street Journal*. Listed as one of the 10 most powerful Spiritual Women in the World. Her students are famous the world over.

E-mail: info@terrycolewhittaker.com

Website: www.terrycolewhittaker.com

Rev. Carolyn Crane is the founder-minister of the Unity Center of Infinite Possibilities in Mobile, Alabama. For more than 30 years, she has been a teacher of the wisdom of possibility thinking, and has proven its value through many personal "opportunities," such as devastating illness (stroke), family deaths, and massive weight loss. Devoted to the respect of all of life, she encourages her students to find, and appreciate, the beauty and joy of each moment; to live life with gentle humor and the sweet love of Spirit. She emphasizes that how we live our lives is a choice.

Unity Center of Infinite Possibilities

5859 Cottage Hill Road

Mobile, Alabama 36609

Phone: 251-661-1788

Weekly Online Newsletter,

  Heart Talk: Unitymob@aol.com

Personal website: www.inthespirit.net

Website: www.unityofmobile.com

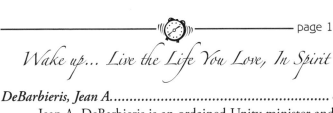

Wake up... Live the Life You Love, In Spirit

Jean A. DeBarbieris is an ordained Unity minister and, with her husband, Skip, a late-in-life adoptive parent. She is passionate about being a mom, and an enthusiastic advocate for international adoption. She is also a gifted speaker, who delights in seeing and sharing the spiritual side of everyday life.
E-mail: chrysalis-spirit@comcast.net

Medical Management Specialist
Phone: 559-297-1070
Fax: 559-297-5517
E-mail: ldowd@pacbell.net

Best-selling author and lecturer
Author of Real Magic, Manifesting Your Destiny, Pulling Your Own Strings and other books.
Website: www.waynedyer.com

Rev. Rudy A. England is the Pastor of Christ in You Fellowship, an interdenominational church in Clear Lake (Houston), Texas. Utilizing his education and skills as a successful, former business and environmental trial lawyer, Rev. England teaches and inspires people to be true to their own life's purpose. He is a husband, father, and ordained minister and counselor.
Christ in You Fellowship
2437 Bay Area Blvd. No. 250
Houston, TX 77058
Phone: 281-474-2491
Website: www.ciyf.org

Wake up... Live the Life You Love, In Spirit

Rev. Susan is the Senior Minister at Unity of Louisville, where the vision is a loving community, awakening humanity to its spiritual magnificence, realizing Oneness with God. Unity is a Christian denomination, publishers of DAILY WORD. Rev. Susan is married to Rev. Jack Poole, ordained Unity minister.

Unity of Louisville
757 S. Brook Street
Louisville, KY 40203
Phone: 502-583-5559
Website: www.unityoflouisville.org

Extraordinary Success with author Anne Marie Evers! Anne Marie Evers is the author of many books and Children's Programs on the Power of Affirmations. She has worked in the personal growth field for many years, teaching and conducting workshops in the following areas: The power of Affirmations, Children's Affirmations, Creative Visualization, Goal-Setting, Positive Thinking, Self-Esteem, How to Attract the Perfect, Lasting, Successful Career, Lasting, Loving Relationship, Optimum Health and much more.

4559 Underwood Avenue,
North Vancouver, B. C.
V7K 2S3 Canada
Phone: 604-988-9907
Fax: 604-904-1127
Email: annemarieevers@shaw.ca
Website: www.affirmations-doctor.com

Wake up... Live the Life You Love, In Spirit

Janette is an ordained minister, speaker, trainer, coach and author. She was the founding minister of the Church for Today in Fresno, CA. She now owns and operates Empowered Living Productions, which creates seminars, workshops and products for empowering the highest potential in individuals. Her passion is inspiring people to awaken to their highest nature, and empowering them to demonstrate and express their deepest dreams. She is committed to living in joy and inspires others to do the same.

She is also the author of *Why Did This Happen to Me Again? Your Keys to Lasting Transformation.*

To receive your FREE REPORT on the "4 KEYS to Developing Courage" please go to Dr. Freeman's website at www.janettemariefreeman.com, Email: revnette@comcast.net

Rev. Margaret ("Margee") Grounds received her ordination from Unity in 1992, and served her first ministry in Savannah, Georgia, for 11 years. After a sabbatical, she moved to Lake Havasu City, Arizona, where she pioneered a Unity ministry which began holding services in February 2005. Margee writes a weekly inspirational column which appears in the Friday edition of the Havasu News-Press. She was awarded her bachelor's degree from Indiana University and her masters from the University of Notre Dame. Her advanced degrees are in English Literature. She lived in South Bend, Indiana, where she was born, for close to 50 years, and held a variety of positions – including teacher of writing, research assistant, newspaper copy editor, and purchasing agent. Unity is precious to her because it was her path to learning the meaning of "You shall know the truth, and the truth shall set you free." You can contact Margee online at imargee@frontiernet.net or by phone at 928-486-9231. The church's website is www.unityofhavasu.org and her mailing address for the church is:

2001 Magnolia #6
Lake Havasu City, AZ 86403   Phone: 928-453-2081

Reverend Trish Hall, an Ordained Religious Science Minister, is the Community Spiritual Leader of the Celebration Center of Religious Science serving the nation's capital from Falls Church, Virginia. Previously she founded the Spiritual Enrichment Center of the Ozarks in Springfield, Missouri, which serves Southwest Missouri and Northwest Arkansas through its center in Springfield, Missouri, and its outreach study groups. In addition to her Master of Divinity, Rev. Hall holds a BA in Counseling with certifications in bereavement counseling, interactive imagery therapy, and neuro-linguistics.

Her personal mission is "I am a beneficial presence in the world, communicating the message of Oneness in such a way as to pass through prejudices and go beyond other limiting beliefs in order to demonstrate how—through the embodiment of the Principles of Science of Mind and Spirit—life can be experienced richly and fully. Blending authenticity, humor and compassion, while always remaining cognizant of Spirit in, as, around, through and throughout all of life—I live the Truth and support others in their personal growth and spiritual transformation.

Celebration Center of Religious Science
2830 Graham Road
Falls Church, Virginia 22042
Phone: 703-560-2030
E-mail: rev-trish@verizon.net

Wake up... Live the Life You Love, In Spirit

Reverend Evelyn Hammond is from Waukegan, Illinois, hometown of Jack Benny. She also uses the age of 39 just as Jack Benny did, and claims it's handed down to the people who are born in Waukegan.

WH Church of RS
21777 Ventura Blvd.
Woodland Hills, CA 91364
1-818-883-1300
E-mail: revevwhcrs@netzero.com
Website: www.wonpower.com

Life is not measured by the number of breaths we take, but by the moments that take our breath away.

Unity minister, Reverend Robin Haruna, lives on the beautiful southern Oregon coast where she has served as minister of Unity Church of Bandon for over ten years. She is author of *The Ten Commitments: Entering the Promised Land of Abundant Life*, in which she reframes "shalt nots" into positive commitments that transform lives.

P.O. Box 518
Bandon, OR 97411
Email: revrobin@haruna.com
Website: www.unityofbandon.org

Dr. Kathy Hearn is the Community Spiritual Leader at the United Church of Religious Science.

2600 West Magnolia Blvd
Burbank, CA 91505
Office: 818-526-7757
E-mail: revkathy@revkathy.com

Wake up... Live the Life You Love, In Spirit

Julie is currently minister and teacher at the Center for Creative Living in Placerville, California. She is also the program director and facilitator for After the Diagnosis, a retreat for women with breast cancer presented by the Lifestyle Education Institute through a grant from the Komen Foundation. A former hospice chaplain, she has worked in end-of-life care for over 15 years. She is a sought-after speaker and facilitator who brings humor, compassion and deep respect for life to all that she does. Julie is co-author of *Caregiver Therapy*, available through Abbey Press.

Website: www.julieinterrante.com

Reverend Bernette Lee Jones is the Senior Minister of the One God One Thought Center for Better Living (OGOT) in Baltimore, Maryland, a New Thought Christian Church; a member of the Universal Foundation for Better Living. Reverend Bernette is also a teacher, writer, motivational speaker, radio talk show host, workshop and retreat facilitator. She has an extensive background working with community based organizations, developing innovative, principle based model programs that address urban issues. Her current work in progress, Conscious Life Design, is a customized, principle based living system that empowers people to live consciously and intentionally on purpose. Her dynamic and thought provoking ministry is committed to forwarding personal, family and community transformation.

Phone: 410-496-5188.
Website: www.onegodonethought.org
E-mail: onethought@aol.com

Wake up... Live the Life You Love, In Spirit

In the field of religion, Dr. Barbara is known as a minister with an extraordinary gift. She has the ability to provide leadership through example and instruction, but more importantly, she is known as a spiritual healer and a truth motivator. The Reverend Dr. Barbara Lewis King is the Founder/Minister of the Hillside Chapel and Truth Center, Inc., in Atlanta, Georgia. Beyond her speaking engagements, she is the author of seven books and monologues.

When asked what she would like to be remembered for, today and in her years to come, Dr. Barbara said: "For my personal commitment to touch someone's life and help them to see their very special talent to be given to the world as only they can."

Hillside Chapel & Truth Center, Inc.
2450 Casade Road, S.W.
Atlanta, GA 30311
Office: 404-472-1929
Fax: 404-472-9882

A highly sought-after speaker, author, and workshop leader, David Laughray has a Ph.D. in psychology, a Doctor of Divinity Degree and is the recognized leader on the psychology of change. He is a life-objective visionary, a ground-breaking leadership strategist and has been a creative career coach to many celebrities and highly respected business leaders.

"The most memorable career coaching experience of my life" — Donald Trump.

A free subscription to Dr. Laughray's "5 part Greatness-Key mini-course," as well as other exciting personal and corporate growth products, are available at: www.awakenyourgreatness.com

Phone: 949-713-9820

Dyanne Maurer, (Professor of comparative religions, actress, motivational speaker), officiates weddings/re-statements everywhere. "The Musical Ceremony" with husband Reverend Howard is unique. Las Vegas based, they're known as "A Scenic Outdoor Wedding."
E-mail: i2loveyou@coam.net
Website: www.ascenicwedding.com

Author of the upcoming book *The Unorthodox Life: Walking the Direct Path to the Divine*
Unity Minister
Unity Temple of Santa Cruz
407 Broadway
Santa Cruz, CA 95060
Phone: 831-423-8553
E-mail: kalm12@aol.com
Website: www.unitysantacruz.org

Dr. Michelle Medrano found Religious Science as a teenager and it changed her life, and helped her find her life path. She served on the administrative staff of Mile Hi Church in Denver, Colorado and as an Assistant Minister at the Huntington Beach Church of Religious Science in Huntington Beach, California. In December of 1995, she became the Community Spiritual Leader of New Vision Spiritual Growth Center in Scottsdale, Arizona. Her passion as a Spiritual Leader is to inspire people to find their spiritual path as directed from within them, and follow that path as a guide to support their most mundane to largest decisions and choices. She is a visionary and powerful speaker who uses her sense of humor and personal examples to lead and uplift others.
E-mail: rev@newvision.org

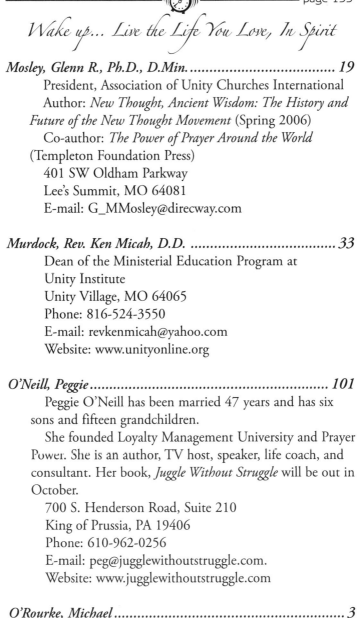

Wake up... Live the Life You Love, In Spirit

For your free gift, go to: **www.wakeupand.com**

Wake up... Live the Life You Love, In Spirit

Best Selling Author, Speaker, Entrepreneur. Don is known throughout the eBay community as The Big Ticket Ace. At any given time he can be found selling Missile Silos, 727 Airplane Homes, Personal Hurricane Bunkers, Private Islands and Inflatable Churches. Don has been profiled in numerous books, TV shows, radio and a multitude of magazines and newspapers.
San Antonio, TX
Phone: 210-349-5892
E-mail: don@InfoBonus.com
Websites: www.iwillsellyourstuff.com
www.bigticketace.com
www.infobonus.com
www.apachebillet.com

Georgia is the founding minister of the Center for Spiritual Awareness, a United Church of Religious Science in Sacramento, CA. She is also a founding member of Lavender Roses, a readers' theater dedicated to the wisdom of Ernest Holmes who wrote, "unity is expressed in multiplicity."
Website: www.centerforspiritualawareness-sacramento.org

The Millionaire Mentor
The # 1 best-selling author and radio personality, Gregory Scott Reid has become known for his energy and candor on the speakers' platform and for his signature phrase, "Always Good!" An experienced entrepreneur in his own right, he is as an effective leader and coach. He is known as "The Millionaire Mentor."
Phone: 877-303-3304
Websites: www.AlwaysGood.com
www.misterkeynote.com

Wake up... Live the Life You Love, In Spirit

Paul is a business development and marketing specialist. His company Aftermedia, Inc. helps authors, speakers, coaches, and leading experts create additional product lines and profit centers. Visit www.aftermedia.com/mye for a complimentary subscription to his "Monetize Your Expertise" newsletter.

Steven E
Creator of the number one best-selling series, *Wake Up...Live the Life You Love.*
E-mail: stevene@wakeuplive.com

Ruth Wallace is an ordained Unity Minister, speaker, trainer, author and coach, as well as a mother and grandmother. She has spoken and taught throughout California, the Midwest and the South. She has contributed to more than 50 books in print and writes a regular newspaper column. She lived and traveled in Europe for three years; and although she butchers two foreign languages, she is fluent in English.
Unity at the Lake at South Lake Tahoe
PO Box: 10742
South Lake, Tahoe 96158
Phone: 530-544-2266
Email: ruthwallace@emailunity.org
Website: unityatthelake.org

Denise is the Senior Minister at Unity Church for
Positive Living in Nashville, Tennessee. She is the mother
of two sons in middle school. Denise's background is in
Child Development and Family Therapy. She also has
degrees in Music and Drama and uses those tools in her
work with individuals and groups. As an NLP Master
Practitioner, Denise has experience working with persons
who want to change the way they think, thereby changing
their lives.

E-mail: denisey@comcast.net